Praise for
Ten Secrets for the Man in the Mirror

Lordship—"Submission to the lordship of Jesus Christ is one of the fundamental keys to leading a happy, fulfilling Christian life. Patrick Morley makes this truth wonderfully clear."

BILL MCCARTNEY, FOUNDER AND PRESIDENT, PROMISE KEEPERS

Balance—"Balance in life comes from making long-term decisions to be structurally sound, not seeking short-term comfort. If you struggle with equilibrium, you've come to the right place!"

ROBERT WOLGEMUTH, BEST-SELLING AUTHOR OF *DADDY@WORK* AND *SHE CALLS ME DADDY*

Vocation—"Everybody 'knows' that success is not enough to satisfy a human soul. Here's a well-written guide for those seeking the path to significance."

BOB BUFORD, FOUNDER OF THE LEADERSHIP NETWORK AND AUTHOR OF *HALFTIME*

Suffering—"Suffering is not God's cataclysmic mistake; it's his way of helping us to truly know him. Patrick Morley will help you to understand how suffering and happiness can be miraculously compatible."

DAVE DRAVECKY, FOUNDER OF DAVE DRAVECKY'S OUTREACH OF HOPE
AND BEST-SELLING AUTHOR AND SPEAKER

Stewardship—"Financial stewardship is almost always a demonstration of a man's life priorities. Patrick Morley helps you understand this truth."

RONALD BLUE, AUTHOR OF *MASTER YOUR MONEY*

Witnessing—"Patrick Morley has been a dear friend for many years. His zeal and the nuggets of truth in this book could profoundly help you be a more effective witness for our Savior."

DR. BILL BRIGHT, FOUNDER AND PRESIDENT OF CAMPUS CRUSADE FOR CHRIST

Service—"The Christian walk is marked by faith and service. These two are inseparable companions. Patrick Morley will help you to clearly understand this unmistakable biblical mandate."

MILLARD FULLER, FOUNDER AND PRESIDENT, HABITAT FOR HUMANITY INTERNATIONAL

Humor—"Patrick Morley and Mary Poppins have something in common. They both understand the power of a spoonful of sugar. Lighten up!"

KEN DAVIS, BEST-SELLING AUTHOR AND SPEAKER

Love—"Inside every man I know is a small boy, longing to be understood, to be heard, to be honored, to be loved. This book will help you learn to love and receive love as well."

GARY SMALLEY, BEST-SELLING AUTHOR OF *MAKING LOVE LAST FOREVER*

Resources by Patrick Morley

Devotions for Couples

The Man in the Mirror

The Rest of Your Life

Second Wind for the Second Half

Second Wind for the Second Half audio

The Seven Seasons of a Man's Life

Ten Secrets for the Man in the Mirror

Ten Secrets for the Man in the Mirror audio

Walking with Christ in the Details of Life

What Husbands Wish Their Wives Knew About Men

What Husbands Wish Their Wives Knew About Men audio

TEN
SECRETS
for the Man in the Mirror

Startling Ideas About
True Happiness

PATRICK MORLEY

ZondervanPublishingHouse
Grand Rapids, Michigan

A Division of HarperCollinsPublishers

We want to hear from you. Please send your comments about this book to us in care of the address below. Thank you.

ZondervanPublishingHouse
Grand Rapids, Michigan 49530
http://www.zondervan.com

Ten Secrets for the Man in the Mirror
Copyright © 2000 by Patrick M. Morley

Requests for information should be addressed to:

ZondervanPublishingHouse
Grand Rapids, Michigan 49530

Library of Congress Cataloging-in-Publication Data

Morley, Patrick M.
    Ten secrets for the man in the mirror: startling ideas about true happiness /
Patrick Morley.
        p. cm.
    Includes bibliographical references.
    ISBN: 0-310-22897-2
    1. Christian men—Religious life. 2. Happiness—Religious aspects—Christianity.
I. Title.
BV4528.2.M69 1999
248.8'42—dc21   99-39363
                                                                                      CIP

This edition is printed on acid-free paper.

Published in association with Wolgemuth and Associates, Inc., PMB 106, 330 Franklin Road #135A-106, Brentwood, TN 37027.

Interior design by Amy E. Langeler

Printed in the United States of America

00 01 02 03 04 05/❖ DC/ 10 9 8 7 6 5 4 3 2 1

To Ken Moar—
my friend and fellow pilgrim for a quarter century. In our
weekly meetings we've scaled spiritual peaks and trudged through
valleys which seemed to cast shadows of death. How comforting to
look back and see that God was making us, not breaking us.

-Contents-

-Introduction-

There's a wonderful story about an entire assembly line at a small factory that shut down when an important piece of machinery broke down.

After several hours the foreman and his crew still couldn't figure out what had gone wrong, so they placed an emergency call to a high-powered consultant. An hour later he arrived, walked around the machine several times, paused, and rubbed his chin thoughtfully.

Then he picked up a hammer, confidently walked over to the machine, tapped it once, and the machine sputtered to life. It groaned to gain rpms while the crew looked on, wondering if the straining machine would make it. Finally, it began to whir and purr, the conveyor belts began to turn again, and the crew let out a loud cheer.

Pure, unadulterated pleasure surged through the consultant as the machine began to hum. On his way out, the happy consultant left a bill for $1,000. When the foreman saw it, he hit the ceiling and demanded an itemized invoice. A couple of days later the expanded invoice arrived:

For tapping the machine: $1

For knowing where to tap: $999

Finding happiness is a lot like fixing that machine. If you don't know where to tap, you won't be happy. The secret is to know where to tap. In this book we'll take a careful look at where to tap in order to find true and lasting happiness.

I don't know of a single man who doesn't want to be happy and successful. Every man wants to lead a more happy, fulfilling, satisfying life. No man wakes up in the morning and thinks, "Well, I wonder what I can do today to make myself unhappy." Yet, sadly, many end up doing just that.

You can see them sitting next to you at any traffic light in America. The pace has numbed their senses. They don't get enough rest. They're always on the fly. They rarely pause to reflect. They do not often sense the presence of God.

Ironically, they spend decades getting what they want, only to find out it doesn't make them happy. They have the outward appearance of success, but the inward agony of spiritual and emotional fatigue. They have success but no peace, things but no pleasure, meaningful work but no gratitude for it, money but no vision to serve others, and relationships but no time to enjoy them. They are unbalanced—unstable, actually—and a high risk to themselves, their families, and their God.

The real problem is, however, that a few moments after we finish looking at them, they look over at us thinking similar thoughts.

Oranges grow in dozens of varieties. The flavor of one orange, however, towers above all the rest. During January and February here in Florida, savvy citrus connoisseurs seek out the quietly famous Honey Bell orange. It is an orange without peer.

The soft skin readily peels from the meat of the fruit, except that the juice squirts all over you as you peel it. As you bite into a mouthwatering section you are overcome by one of the most succulent textures and tastes you've ever put in your mouth. The sweet nectar stimulates your salivary glands. Peace sweeps over your whole being as you realize that you have just experienced a pleasure that cannot be duplicated. Once you've tasted a Honey Bell orange, it's difficult— nearly impossible—to ever again be satisfied by any ordinary orange.

And that's how it is with God. Once you've tasted the excellencies of Jesus and the joy of his kingdom, it would be difficult to ever again be satisfied with any ordinary happiness.

In this book we will explore ten secrets of happiness for men who want to be happy but have not yet figured out, or perhaps once knew but have now forgotten, exactly where to tap. Here's my hope for you— that by the end of this book you will have tasted God in such a way that you could never again be satisfied with any ordinary happiness.

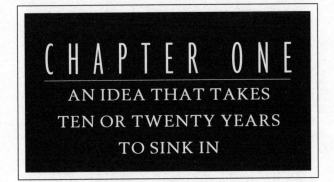

CHAPTER ONE

AN IDEA THAT TAKES TEN OR TWENTY YEARS TO SINK IN

An Idea That Takes Ten or Twenty Years to Sink In

Once upon a time there lived a master who owned a great estate. One day he learned that a scruffy mongrel dog at the local animal shelter had been scheduled for destruction. Gripped by compassion, the master had his servants bring the mangy animal into his home and clean it up.

As you can imagine, the mutt was suddenly most happy. The master called his new dog into the study where he was going over a few affairs pertaining to his great estate, though the dog knew little of what the master owned or did. With his large, strong hand the master reached down to pet and comfort his new companion and friend.

The dog was a mixed breed, but he was intelligent. Though not fully understanding the benevolent act of his new master, Petros (for that was now his name) was overwhelmed with gratitude. He returned the master's kindness by licking his hand. This made the master feel warm and loving toward his new possession. "I love you very much," he said, "and everything I have here is for your enjoyment. The yard where you can run and play is large. I will make sure you are always well fed, and you can come and sit by my side any time you want. I will protect you and watch over you from now on." These promises made Petros swell with joy.

"I do have a few rules, though," added the master, "which you should obey. First, I have other dogs I have brought home over the years, and you must love them like I do and not quarrel with them. There's plenty of food for all of you—and more than enough land to share.

"Second, I will from time to time ask you to welcome other dogs I bring home and teach them the things you learn about what it means to belong to me. Also, everybody here has work to do, so you will need to do your fair share. That's about it, really, but I want to say again that I would love to spend as much time with you as I can. Oh, by the way, stay inside the fence I've built. It's for your own protection. Beyond the fence are many dangers to dogs, and I want to spare you from any more hardships than you've already experienced."

With this, the happy dog trotted out into the sunny yard and took a deep breath, thankful to his new master for his mercy toward such a dog. He could not believe his good fortune. He thought to himself, *You know, I had heard about this place and wondered, Wouldn't it be nice if it were true? But I didn't believe it really existed.*

Over the next several months Petros began to get to know the other dogs the master had collected. It was a motley, unseemly lot. He couldn't seem to find any pattern at all to how his master chose his dogs. They were of many colors, big and little, pedigreed and mutt, male and female. They were from all walks of life, actually. The only common denominator he could find was the master who had taken them in and loved them.

Many of the more experienced dogs taught Petros about the ways of his master. But he was surprised to learn that a number of the other dogs no longer appreciated all the master had done to save them. In fact, some actually grumbled and complained that the yard wasn't big enough and that the food was always the same. It was widely discussed among these disgruntled dogs that life outside the boundaries of the master's estate was far more exciting. Each year a number of dogs would actually dig under the fence and run away.

The runaway dogs were rarely heard from again, but the general consensus among the remaining dogs was that the runaways were better off. Actually, nothing could have been further from the truth. Life on the outside was cruel. Most of the dogs ran in packs, so it was dangerous to be outside the fence on your own. The provisions of the forest couldn't match those of the master's kitchen, and the packs of dogs often fought with each other for territory and for access to the limited resources of the forest.

Perhaps the only reason the forest dogs could survive at all was because piles of food, mostly scraps, mysteriously appeared from time to time. Unbeknownst to the forest dogs, the master of the estate regularly had his servants take scraps from his table and, under cloak of darkness, put them out for the runaways.

The more the new dog talked with the malcontented dogs about what they didn't like, the more he questioned the motives of his master. The more he questioned, the less time he spent licking the master's hand and feeling the warmth of the master's hand stroking his coat of hair. Whenever he did go to see the master, though, the owner of the estate was consistently delighted to see him and always asked how he was doing. The master would stop whatever he was doing to focus on the dog. Yet, over a period of time Petros's mind fantasized about the adventures that must lie on the other side of the fence. Curiosity gave way to desire; desire became longing; longing became lust.

Over time the dog's lust for the forest grew and grew until one day it finally outweighed his desire for the master's care. He had heard a rumor that several other discontented dogs planned to tunnel under the fence and run away. After some hesitation, he decided to join the rebellion, and that night he scampered through the hole to what he thought would be glorious freedom from the master's unbending rules.

Once all the dogs had made their way through the hole, they couldn't agree on who would be their leader, so they all separated and went in their own directions. Petros was shocked at how quickly the group fell apart. He found a place under the stars to spend the night, but he couldn't help missing the warm blanket by the master's hearth where he had always slept before.

Early the next morning he awakened, glad he no longer had to obey the master, happy he was now his own master.

Most of the forest had been carved up into territories by the other dogs, and Petros figured he would have to cast his lot with one pack or another if he was going to become the dog he'd always dreamed of becoming.

He traveled about the forest, meeting different types of dog packs. Some seemed bent on taking advantage of the other packs and plotted what seemed to him to be evil schemes. He wanted nothing to do with that. Others were noticeably industrious and were building estates of their own. It appeared they were trying to imitate the estate of the master. Packs competed with each other to see who could create the most beautiful estate in the forest, though their successes were limited. One pack eyed another, and envy appeared to be the chief motivation of all they did.

A few of the dog packs picked leaders who seemed determined to imitate the master of the estate. They encouraged the dogs in their packs to lick their paws and pay them tribute, just the way they used to do for the master.

Whether the dogs were in an evil pack, an envious pack, or a religious pack, Petros noticed that the longer the dogs had been away from the master's estate the more sickly they appeared to be. It was as though, regardless of their material success in the forest, their souls hungered for something they could only get on the grounds of the estate. At first, Petros couldn't put his paw on exactly what it was.

Suddenly one day it dawned on him. He remembered the happy feelings of love, peace, and joy that used to come over him when he

licked his master's hand. He had found such pleasure in paying tribute
to the master for his kindness. He deeply enjoyed the happiness he had
felt when the master stroked him. All at once, he realized how much
the touch of the master's hand had meant to him and to all these other
runaway dogs.

Soon he too began to lose weight, and he began to remember again
those lonely days before he had ever known the master.

When Petros didn't return after several days, the master was heartbroken that he had run away. Each day at sunrise the master would
walk to the gate of his estate and look in the direction of the forest. He
would call the name he had given his dog, hoping he might appear and
come home.

So heartbroken was the master that he soon organized a search
party of his servants to look through the forest. One day, the servants
found Petros and tried to coax him from the tiny cave where he was living. All day long they tried to persuade the dog that the master deeply
loved him and wanted him to come home. But Petros, even though
lonely and hungry, couldn't bring himself to admit he had made a mistake. He had believed the lies about the master the other runaway dogs
had spread around. He still mistakenly thought the master's rules sti-
fled his freedom, and so by nightfall the servants gave up and returned
to the master with their dreary report.

It was on that day that a great tug of war began within the dog. On
the one paw, the forest was a great hub of activity. Petros was enamored
with the world of the forest. Here it was, he thought, that he could
become the dog he had always wanted to be. Yet, on the other paw, he
saw how disillusioned and emaciated the souls of the forest dogs were,
who, ironically, couldn't seem to see what was wrong with them. In fact,
some of the most reckless dogs acted like they were the ones who most
had it together.

Petros began to see that in order for a dog to be happy, he needed
more than merely allowing the master to save him. He needed to come
under the long-term care and protection of the master. The forest was

a mean and hard place because it deceived a dog into thinking he needed to get his own way to be happy.

The great tug of war continued for some years to come. Occasionally a search party of servants would find Petros and ask if he was ready to come home, but he always resisted.

What the dog couldn't know, however, was that the master's estate included not only the property inside the fence, but he owned the forest as well. Ironically, all the runaway dogs were nothing more than squatters on the master's land. Yet, the master was gracious, and even though they had rejected him, he continued to provide for their care, albeit in a much more limited way, by letting them use the forest they thought was theirs. They simply didn't understand that he owned everything as far as the eye could see. He was the lord of all.

Ideas That Take Ten or Twenty Years to Sink In

In life we learn many lessons in brilliant flashes of insight. Other lessons, though, seep in over the course of many years.

For example, from the first moment the thought broke into my mind that "prayer is the most important thing I can do," it took another twenty years to expel the thought that "there are better ways to go about getting things done." And like a nearly empty tube of toothpaste, you can never quite squeeze out the old thought completely.

In a similar way, I remember the first time I caught a glimpse of the idea "I can rely on God" as it scampered through my mind. Even though I came to believe it unyieldingly, it took another twenty years to back the old thought "I can do it on my own" into a corner and pin his arms so he couldn't take a swing at me. Still today I can see that smirking "old man" standing over there in the corner, calling out to me, asking for just one more chance to prove he's right.

There is another idea that has only recently been sinking in for me and grabbing me at the core of my being. Personally, I believe it's one of the greatest lessons I've ever learned. I believe it is the golden secret to success. I believe it is "the first and the last word" on happiness. It is the essence of what it means to declare Jesus Christ as Lord. This idea may resonate with you as soon as you hear it, or you may recoil from it at first. You may even disagree with it. Yet, I believe it is the one idea in this book that can most change your life and my life. So, you may want to read it carefully …

THE CHRISTIAN LIFE IS A BROAD ROAD OF HAPPINESS, JOY, PEACE, BLESSING, SUCCESS, SIGNIFICANCE, AND CONTENTMENT, WHICH IS IRONICALLY GAINED BY CHOOSING THE NARROW ROAD OF SURRENDER, OBEDIENCE, SELF-DENIAL, SELF-SACRIFICE, TRUTH, WORSHIP, AND SERVICE.

Let's unpack this idea a little bit. The world would say, "Want to be happy? Seek a better job. Live in this neighborhood. Take this vacation. Drive this car. Send your children to this school. Accumulate this much money. Join this club." God says, "Want to be happy? Surrender your life to me. Obey me. Seek the truth. Live by faith. Give yourself away in service. Deny yourself."

Jesus does reward, but as early-twentieth-century writer Bruce Barton observed, Jesus used the higher style of leadership that brings forth a man's greatest effort not by the picture of great rewards but by the promise of obstacles. Author Dallas Willard notes in *The Divine Conspiracy* that Jesus "links" the broad road of abundance to the narrow road of obedience.

Ironically, when we yield our lives to Jesus, bring ourselves under his authority, allow him to be Lord (which he is regardless), and walk in his way of obedience, service, and self-denial—things that sound like giving up happiness—he rewards us with every spiritual blessing. He links the broad road of abundance to the narrow road of obedience.

Recently I found myself writing these words in my journal: "God, it is in your plan, purpose, and will that I find these pleasant things. Your will is agreeable with me. Ours is not a contest to get around, manipulate, or overcome your will, but to enter in. It is not a roadblock, but a gate."

Happiness and Truth

Happiness is linked to truth. Some things are true, whether we choose to believe them or not. Suppose for a moment you had a headache. Let's say someone gave you a pill that contained rat poison but told you it was an aspirin. Let's also say that you sincerely believed them. If you take the pill will you be happy? Dead, maybe, but definitely not happy. That's because the truth is what it is. You can be sincere, but sincerely wrong.

The Christian life is not built on feelings or impressions that shift from one generation to the next. Rather, it is based on the historical life, death, and resurrection of Jesus Christ and the faith life revealed in the Bible. Jesus prayed, "Sanctify them by the truth; your word is truth" (John 17:17). To be happy we must be seekers of truth. The Bible says, "True worshipers will worship the Father in spirit and truth, for they are the kind of worshipers the Father seeks" (John 4:23). Incidentally, the word *worship* has at the core of its meaning "to kiss, the way a dog licks its master's hand." It is on the narrow road of truth and worship that we find the broad road of happiness.

Joy and Obedience

Jesus links joy to obedience. Jesus said, "If you obey my commands, you will remain in my love, just as I have obeyed my Father's commands and remain in his love. I have told you this so that my joy may be in you and that your joy may be complete" (John 15:10–11).

Also, blessing is linked to obedience. "As Jesus was saying these things, a woman in the crowd called out, 'Blessed is the mother who gave you birth and nursed you.' He replied, 'Blessed rather are those who hear the word of God and obey it'" (Luke 11:27–28). It is on the narrow road of humble submission and obedience to God's will that we find the broad road of joy and blessing.

Happiness and Self-Denial

Happiness is linked to self-denial. My work entails frequent airplane travel. When I am greeted at the gate upon arrival at my destination the question I'm most often asked—a way, I suppose, of breaking the ice—is, "How was your flight?"

Because frequent air travel ranks among the five most boring activities ever known to mankind, this is a difficult question on which to start a friendship. From my perspective, I've just wobbled up a steaming-hot Jetway after stepping off a freezing-cold jet plane. I'd be completely dehydrated, except for the fact that I drink eight ounces of water for every one hour I spend in flight. This means that if I don't find a rest room within sixty seconds of deplaning, the scream I've been working so hard to suppress will bring airport security rushing at me from all directions with outstretched arms.

The constant motion of an airplane makes you queasy, some kid is always crying, your neighbor either talks too much or has a cold (or both), the flight attendants try hard but invariably bump your elbow with the service cart, every time you go up and come down you use up about twenty-five percent of your available energy for that day (fifty percent if you have to make a connection), and the words "on-time flight" constitute an aviation oxymoron. Air travel is the ultimate form of self-denial (and masochism, I might add). So, possessing a compulsion to give a straightforward answer, I've always struggled with that question, "How was your flight?"

I usually answer, "Well, as the Lord Jesus said, 'If any man would come after me he must deny himself, take up his cross, and fly with me.'" It does break the ice.

This is how the Lord actually put it: "If anyone would come after me, he must deny himself and take up his cross daily and follow me. For whoever wants to save his life will lose it, but whoever loses his life for me will save it. What good is it for a man to gain the whole world, and yet lose or forfeit his very self?" (Luke 9:23–25).

It is on the narrow road of self-denial that we find the broad road of success and peace.

Happiness and Service

Happiness is linked to serving others. Jesus said, "Whoever serves me must follow me; and where I am, my servant also will be. My Father will honor the one who serves me" (John 12:26). The broad road of honor, contentment, and lasting significance ironically comes when we travel the narrow road of serving others.

All men want to be happy. The truth of this statement is so obvious that it barely needs mentioning. Yet men often fail to discover the one sure path to happiness. Happiness does not consist in getting what we want. The most famous of all wise men, Solomon, proved that hap-

SECRET #1
LORDSHIP

You have probably heard someone say, or maybe have yourself said, "Jesus was my Savior but not my Lord." Nothing could be more wrong! He is always the Lord and always has been. He is the Lord of all men at all times in all places, whether they acknowledge it or not. As Lord, Jesus is the *creator* and *sustainer* of all men (even those who spurn his name) and, as Savior, the *redeemer* of those who believe. We belong to Jesus. He is our "owner." He is our "benefactor." In fact, he is our Lord whether he is our Savior or not.

piness does not come from merely getting what you want. Rather, happiness is built on the foundation of acknowledging that Jesus Christ is the Lord of our lives. The path to happiness is the one that leads back to the master's estate. He's standing at the gate to say, "I've missed you. Welcome home."

Consider these Bible verses:

◆ **For there is no difference between Jew and Gentile — the same Lord is Lord of all and richly blesses all who call on him (Romans 10:12).**

◆ **For this very reason, Christ died and returned to life so that he might be the Lord of both the dead and the living (Romans 14:9).**

◆ **And there is but one Lord, Jesus Christ, through whom all things came and through whom we live (1 Corinthians 8:6).**

◆ **"Therefore let all Israel be assured of this: God has made this Jesus, whom you crucified, both Lord and Christ" (Acts 2:36).**

◆ **You know the message God sent to the people of Israel, telling the good news of peace through Jesus Christ, who is Lord of all (Acts 10:36).**

◆ **So, whether we live or die, we belong to the Lord (Romans 14:8).**

The question isn't whether or not Jesus is Lord—he is. The question is whether or not we will acknowledge that he is our Lord. Sometimes, like a good son, we cooperate with him. At other times, though, he must intervene and sovereignly orchestrate our circumstances to help us overcome our apathy or rebellion. Thankfully, he is the Lord, and he will never give up on us—even when we think he isn't Lord.

Perhaps you have been pursuing happiness down a wrong road. Perhaps you left the brightness and warmth of the estate for the darkness and chill of the forest. Perhaps you need to let the idea sink deep into both mind and heart that Jesus is Lord. If so, let me encourage you to express your heart to God. Here is a prayer you may find helpful as you consider how to get back on the right road:

> *Dear Lord,*
>
> *I'm tired of eating the scraps. I've settled for so much less than you had planned for me. I thought I would get what I wanted by pursuing my goals. It has not worked out that way. What a stark contrast between the futility, frustration, vanity, and meaninglessness of life "in the forest" and the virtually indescribable joy that comes by walking in humble submission to you, Master Jesus. How I long for your joy, peace, and contentment. It is in your plan, purpose, and will that I find these pleasant things. Your will is agreeable with me. My sin is that I have been in a contest to get around, manipulate, or overcome your will rather than to enter in. I now see that I must take the narrow road of surrender, truth, obedience, faith, service, self-denial, and self-sacrifice. It is not a roadblock, but a gate. Here I stand at the gate. I ask your forgiveness. I am so sorry. Yes, you are the Lord, and I belong to you. Amen.*

FOCUS QUESTIONS

1. **In the illustration of the master and the dog, where on the master's property are you right now — in the house, the yard, or the forest? How long have you been there, and why? Is that where you want to be right now?**

2. **The statement was made that Jesus Christ is the Lord of all men at all times in all places, whether they acknowledge it or not. Do you agree or not? Explain your answer. (Refer to the Bible verses on page 25.)**

3. "The Christian life is a broad road of happiness, joy, peace, blessing, success, significance, and contentment, which is ironically gained by choosing the narrow road of surrender, obedience, self-denial, self-sacrifice, truth, worship, and service." Do you agree or not, and why? Which road are you on? What's your next step?

4. Give an example of something you did to deny yourself that ultimately resulted in a blessing.

CHAPTER TWO

HOW HAPPY DO YOU
HAVE TO BE?

2

How Happy Do You Have to Be?

When you attend a social gathering, how do you answer when someone asks, "How are you doing?"

For decades I cringed when someone would ask this question. The question puts us in an awkward position. It's a social question to which people want a brief, casual answer. But how should we answer it? Should we give a shallow, trite answer? Or should we tell people the truth—the plain, unvarnished truth about how we are really doing—even if we do so only briefly?

One day when asked the question I happened to respond, "I'm busy and balanced." Immediately I thought, *That's it! That's the answer I've been looking for!* For me, it was a moment of clarity. I like being busy. To be busy is a good thing. There is nothing more boring than not being busy.

And yet if you say, "I'm really busy," some will take it to mean you are out of balance. On the other hand, if you are experiencing a pretty good pace in your life and say, "Not too busy," you may feel like you've just announced your availability to take on additional projects—work that almost assuredly *will* push you over the edge.

On this particular day I was "just right" so I answered, "I'm busy and balanced." And that's exactly how I want to live my life. This chapter puts flesh on that idea.

Most of us feel stressed enough to want more balance in our lives, but not stressed enough to downsize. While a less challenging job or a smaller mortgage payment may from time to time sound appealing, any serious consideration invariably leads to the conclusion that it's impractical.

Still the question remains, "How can a busy man lead a more balanced life?" This chapter explores how to stay "balanced" without giving up "busy."

Immediate Comfort or Long-term Support

My feet are flat and I've got bunions. When I speak at a weekend men's event, which I do regularly, my legs and feet get so tired that I can barely stand when it's over. It generally takes two full days to recover.

Over the years I've tried orthopedic inserts and a variety of other remedies. Recently I purchased an expensive pair of orthopedic shoes made in France, which the salesman described as "the best-fitting shoes in the world." When I arrived home, I decided to see how comfortable the new shoes felt in comparison to my existing soft-sole shoes as well as my tennis shoes.

On my left foot I laced up the new shoe. On my right foot I slipped on the old soft-sole shoe. To my surprise, as I walked around the old shoe felt considerably more comfortable than the new one. In a small panic, I replaced the soft-sole shoe with my tennis shoe. That shoe, too, felt considerably more comfortable than the new shoe.

I phoned the salesman at the shoe store and said, "Look, I'm having a little buyer's remorse here," and then I explained what I had done.

"Oh, I think I understand," he said. "The problem is that Americans equate fit with comfort. Europeans, on the other hand, equate fit with the long-term structural support the shoe provides. Even though your other shoes feel more comfortable when you first put them on, by the end of the day they will leave you much more fatigued than the shoes you just purchased.

"You can read more about it in the brochure in the shoe box. Why not wear the shoes around the house or office for the rest of the day and see if you don't like them better in the long run. If you want, however, I will gladly give you a full refund."

Somewhat hesitantly, I agreed to his test. Because I had purchased the shoes a few days before I was to speak at a weekend men's event, I decided to give the shoes a full test that Friday night and Saturday morning. At the end of the event on Saturday, to my surprise and pleasure, I felt like a new man. My legs didn't bother me at all!

In life, we usually decide how happy we are based on how comfortable we are. However, what's immediately comfortable often doesn't provide the long-term structural support we need. What balances a busy life is focusing not so much on immediate comfort but on long-term structural support. Where does that support come from?

How Happy Do You Have to Be?

Ed, the chief financial officer of an 800-employee company, once asked me, "How happy do I have to be in my work?"

"Tell me more," I replied.

"Well," Ed continued, "I've been doing the same thing for thirteen years. Three years ago I went to work for my present employer. I'm making lots of money, but I'm wondering if this is what I want to do. I want to do something significant with my life. I've got an opportunity to go into business for myself, which I'm seriously considering doing."

"What are some of your accomplishments in your present job?" I asked.

"Actually, I've been able to make a significant contribution to my company. I've been able to introduce a first-rate retirement plan. By God's grace we now have a health plan that allows our employees to go to the doctors they want, when they want. And I initiated a number of policy reforms, which have led to our employees treating each other and our customers with more dignity. Morale, they tell me, has never been better."

"So essentially," I said, "your work is going well and you are making a contribution. What about the other areas of your life?"

Ed said, "My wife Edie and I couldn't be happier. We are together on all the major points. My kids seem fine—we do lots of things with them. Spiritually I feel like I'm close to God. But I still don't feel like I'm doing anything significant with my life."

"Ed," I said. "It sounds like most everything is going well, but there is one area you haven't mentioned. What are you doing to serve the Lord?"

After a long pause, Ed said, "Well, you know, it's interesting you ask that very question. Three years ago, before I took this position, I was leading a small group men's Bible study in my church. But I've been so busy these last three years that I basically haven't had any time to serve the Lord."

"Let me see if I can put our conversation in perspective," I said. "You have a good relationship with the Lord, you love your wife and your relationship with her is good, you spend a healthy amount of time with your children, and you've made some key contributions in your work. However, you have not been serving God. You feel like something's missing, so you're considering making a career change."

"That's about it," he said.

Solving the Wrong Problem

"Ed, it may be that the only way to regain a sense of significance is for you to change employers. However, I would like to suggest another possibility. I think it's at least possible that you may be trying to solve the wrong problem.

"The Bible outlines four universal purposes for all men:

◆ **The Great Commandment (Matthew 22:36–38)** — loving God

◆ **The New Commandment (John 13:34)** — loving others

◆ **The Cultural Mandate (Genesis 1:28)** — tending to our work and family

◆ **The Great Commission (Matthew 28:18–20)** — serving God by serving others through evangelism, discipleship, and meeting the needs of the poor

"Our own personal calling is the unique way God weaves particular threads of those four purposes into our particular lives. Unless we strike a right balance among these four purposes, we will not be happy and content. I would like to suggest that your unhappiness at work might actually be from not having a personal ministry.

"Of course no one else can tell you what God's will is for your life, but I have a suggestion for you to consider. Instead of making a work change right now, why not devote the next six months to discovering your spiritual gifts and exploring new avenues to serve God through serving others? Then see if after several months you find joy returning to your work.

"As it is now, though, you may find changing jobs won't actually solve your problem of wanting to do something more significant. However, if after six months of leading a more balanced life you're still discontent, then by all means, make a move."

What is the major decision you are trying to make right now? How can you be sure you are solving the right problem? Much of this book is devoted to helping you make sure you're solving the right problems.

SECRET #2
BALANCE

Every day men make decisions to take a different job, get rid of an old wife, get a new wife, move to another city, buy a bigger house, or trade in their old car for a different car. But a few weeks later the "hole" they were trying to fill seems just as gaping. Why? Because we often end up solving the wrong problem. We can find what we're looking for by striking a right balance between the four universal purposes God has for all men: The Great Commandment, the New Commandment, the Cultural Mandate, and the Great Commission. It is a secret to leading a happy, busy, and balanced life.

Where to Be a Hero

Scott Alexander and I travel together. I speak, he sings. Scott Alexander is not exactly a household name. He is not a recording artist, though he could be. He is not a hero to your kids, because your kids have never heard of him. Why not? Because many years ago Scott decided he would rather be a hero to his own kids.

A lot of what it means to lead a busy but balanced life is as simple as deciding to whom you want to be a hero.

Here's an exercise you may find revealing. Make a list of the top five ways you use your time. Next, make a list of your five most important relationships. Now compare them. Are the ways in which you spend your time actually related to the most important people in your life? If not, what steps might you take to bring them into alignment?

Four Frogs for Fame

It was a sad day when the news arrived that Steven, the chief operating officer of a major stock exchange-listed company, had died suddenly and unexpectedly at the age of fifty-two. Among a handful of the most respected leaders in his industry, even his most hardened, cynical competitors paused to acknowledge a moment of grief.

His job, one of the most coveted in the industry, went unfilled for two years. Eventually the company made an offer to Tom. At the age of fifty, Tom, who had been a close friend of Steven, was honored to receive such a prestigious and lucrative offer.

Yet he and his wife Barbara, who had just finished putting two children through college, felt settled where they were. His consulting business provided a great deal of flexibility, and they had a solid financial future. Still, the prestige and wealth dangling like a piece of bait from a fishing pole were considerable.

Tom and his wife took a long weekend to pray and think things over—what it would mean in lifestyle changes should Tom accept this job offer. Barbara stared deeply into the smile-creased face of the husband she loved so deeply, the man with whom she had faced—and survived—at least a dozen major tests.

Quietly she said, "Having our friend die at fifty-two was one thing. But to take his job, assume his pressures, and make so many sacrifices for the money and prestige…are you sure that's what God would want us to do? Tom, what if you knew today that in two years you, like Steven, would die? Is this the way you would want to spend these next two years?" Barbara's questions hit him hard.

After a gut-wrenching emotional struggle, Tom and Barbara concluded that the right thing to do—the decision that reflected God's will for them—was to turn down the offer. A few months later the position was filled. Steven's young widow, who had moved to another city, returned to clean out her deceased husband's office so the new chief operating officer could move in. While in town, she visited with Tom and Barbara and told them, "I'm so glad you didn't take that job."

Later, Barbara said, "Once you've sat several times in what Solomon called 'the house of mourning,' some things don't seem so important anymore. Right now I'm sitting here at Tom's desk looking out over the pond in our backyard. I see three frogs in the water poking their heads up through the stalks of grass, and one little frog sitting on the bank trying to decide whether or not to jump in. Now why would we ever want to give that up?" Good question!

Part of leading a balanced life means possessing the wisdom to know when watching four frogs at play in your backyard is the most important choice you can make.

FOCUS QUESTIONS

1. **Have you settled the issue of where you want to be a hero? What is your conclusion? What will it take to make it happen?**

2. **Which of the following best describes your life right now? Why?**

   Too Busy   Busy   Busy and Balanced   Balanced   Too Inactive

   What is one practical step you can take to get where you want to be?

3. **Have you thought of happiness as immediate comfort or as long-term structural support? What's the difference in your mind?**

4. **Long-term structural support comes by striking a right balance among the four universal purposes God has for**

all men. Rate how balanced you are in each area (4 =
very balanced, 3 = mostly balanced, 2 = somewhat balanced, 1 = not balanced at all):

___ The Great Commandment — loving God

___ The New Commandment — loving others

___ The Cultural Mandate — tending to our work and
family

___ The Great Commission — serving God by serving
others

What changes, if any, do your ratings suggest you consider?

5. What is the major problem you are trying to solve right
now? What is the chance that you may be trying to
solve the wrong problem? How can you be sure?

CHAPTER THREE

NOT HAPPY HERE,
NOT HAPPY ANYWHERE

3

Not Happy Here,
Not Happy Anywhere

My fiftieth birthday present was a trip to Plains, Georgia, to attend Jimmy Carter's Sunday school class, a class that has been visited by over 55,000 people from eighty countries since 1982.

My wife and I stayed at a bed-and-breakfast inn in nearby Americus. Exploring the downtown area on Saturday morning, I stepped into the local men's clothing store where I purchased a leather coat. George, the store's owner, asked where I was from, and I said, "We're from Florida, up to visit President Carter's Sunday school class tomorrow morning."

"He's a good man. I've enjoyed doing business with him," said George as he disappeared into the back room. He quickly returned with a book autographed by the former president and proudly pointed out the inscription: "To George the tailor." Beaming, he said, "Jimmy Carter always calls me that—'George the tailor.'"

There can be little doubt that we gain a great deal of our identity from our vocation. While what we do is most assuredly not who we are, biblically speaking our vocation does, or should, contribute significantly to our feelings of worth, contribution, and human dignity.

The Situation

When it comes to happiness, few subjects are as important to us as our vocations. Our work is not merely a means to other ends; it is an end in itself. Every honest vocation is noble. Work has intrinsic value. It is not merely a way to feed our appetites for other things.

Meaningful work is a wonderful gift from God. We are created to work, and a man who is unhappy in his work will probably not be happy anywhere. When a man is unhappy in other areas of his life, he can still hold together a semblance of happiness. But he who is unhappy in his work is unhappy everywhere. The man who is unhappy in his work will be unhappy at home, at church, in his relationship with God, and in his general approach to life.

Here's a great tragedy: Because a man who is unhappy in his work is typically unhappy everywhere, he often attempts to solve the wrong problem. He thinks his wife is the problem—so he gets a new wife. He thinks his children are the problem—so he persecutes them with strict rules and regulations and with frequent outbursts of anger. He thinks God doesn't care, so he turns his back on him. In short, he is miserable everywhere because he is miserable in his work, so he typically drags those closest to him into his misery.

By the end of this chapter you will have a better understanding of why men become unhappy in their work. You will also be challenged about what it takes to be happy in your work, both biblically and practically. A number of specific steps on the road to vocational happiness will be outlined.

So the question begs to be asked: How can a man be happy in the work he has? Or, if that's not possible, how can he go about finding work that does make him happy?

Balancing Work with Family

Gary spent the first ten years of his career managing (and turning around) a number of branch offices for his company. As his reward, he was finally offered the position he had always wanted—assistant to the president and chief executive officer of the multibillion-dollar company into which he had poured himself.

However, the promotion required that he move cross-country with his wife and three children—far away from extended family. Now that he finally had what he wanted in his grasp, he wasn't so sure.

He sought counsel from his friends, who said, "What's there to think about?" meaning, "Of course you should go!" His wife also sought counsel from her friends, who said, "What's there to think about?" meaning, "Why would you ever want to do that? Of course you should stay!"

Surely the two largest blocks of time we invest go to family and work. Perhaps our greatest challenge is how to juggle them success-fully. In the end, Gary decided he had moved around enough. His "new breed" company honored his decision, and he has found a deep sense of gratification in continuing to manage a branch office.

Another man may have come to a different conclusion, but Gary felt strongly that he and his wife needed to be "together" on such a major decision. For him, God's will wouldn't be revealed as a "split vote" between him and his wife. In other words, he fully received and respected his wife's opinion as one clear way in which God leads.

A friend recently riveted my attention when he said, "Our ten-dency as men is to compartmentalize that which we shouldn't and not compartmentalize that which we should." He meant that, as men, we tend to compartmentalize our families and set them off in a separate little box over on the side, hardly giving them a thought during the workday. But we tend not to compartmentalize our work. Instead, we bring it home where it occupies our minds through dinner and into the evening. Our bodies are at home, but our minds are at work.

To succeed at work but to fail at home is to fail completely. Striking a right balance between work and family is a cornerstone of achieving true and lasting happiness.

Knowing the Future

At lunch one day, Wendell asked several questions about how to find contentment in his work. During the first forty-five minutes of our meal, he shared a number of ways in which his life had been uniquely blessed. He also shared that he was somewhat frustrated over current circumstances in his life.

Wendell had built his company into a solid entity and then had sold it for a sizable fortune—all cash. He remained with the company as the president and chief executive officer. He has five lovely children who are all doing well. The previous year his wife survived a near-death experience, reviving after being connected to a life-support system for twenty minutes.

As he paused for a few moments in our conversation I asked him, "Are you happy?"

Without hesitation he said, "No."

Many of us suffer the way Wendell suffered. We achieve our goals, we have many wonderful blessings, and yet we still feel unsettled and anxious.

After listening carefully to his story, I was struck by the irony of having so much to be thankful for, yet feeling stalked by the demons of unhappiness.

I found myself blurting out, "You just want to know the future. You want to know how it's all going to turn out. I would suggest that true happiness comes as we learn that the process itself is the purpose. It is not the goal that makes a man happy. On the contrary, the uncertainty about how our goals will turn out only creates anxiety. Rather, it is engaging and enjoying the process of living out our lives day by day—enjoying each step along the way—that makes a man happy."

A few days later Wendell sent a perceptive follow-up note:

> Your comment over lunch, "You just want to know the future," was a healthy bit of criticism. Uncertainty is the degree to which a number of alternatives and probabilities plague my mind. Uncertainty motivates me to seek information. Somehow I have let myself believe that with the "right information" I could control the future outcome of events. With this perspective one loses sight of the fact that the process is the goal. Over the next months I will be pursuing process more diligently. I will also remember that it is God's process, not mine.

Ecclesiastes 7:14 instructs us, "A man cannot discover anything about his future." Yet, ironically, we often spend much of our time stewing over that which we will never know until it happens. Doesn't that seem like a hollow and fruitless use of time? Would it not be more useful to once and for all accept the fact that the future is the secret of God, then live by faith, trusting that because God is good, our future will end "good"? What a comfort to trust, and rest, in the sovereignty of a good God!

On the other hand, trusting God doesn't mean we shouldn't do our "homework." Proverbs 3:5–6 says, "Trust in the LORD with all your heart and *lean not on your own understanding*; in all your ways acknowledge him, and he will make your paths straight" (italics added).

Implicit in the idea of not leaning on "your own understanding" is that you have already gained an understanding on which you are now told not to rely! Trusting God isn't flying blind. Gain an understanding—know your product; study the economic trends; learn the likes and dislikes of your customers; improve your skills. But after you've done all that, don't depend on the "strength" of what you know, but on God.

Happiness in our work depends, negatively, on not stewing over how the future will turn out and, positively, on trusting in God's goodness. If you want to be happy in your work you must somehow move from focusing on "future accomplishment" to "present process."

Finding Your Core Motivation

I have a friend who is motivated by making money. Over the years we have talked about many other motivations. Yet he cannot conceive that anyone is motivated by anything but money.

But what about the motivation of a teacher who loves children, a minister called to shepherd a flock, a retiree who serves others, a student thirsty for knowledge, a small businessman who wants to run his own show, an engineer fascinated by jet propulsion, or downsizers who want a simpler lifestyle?

In the end, they all do possess one universal motivation, but it is not money. It is the desire to find significance, meaning, and dignity in who they are and what they do. This, in the end, defines happiness. All other motivations are means to this one end. Ultimately, significance can only be gained in a lasting way by glorifying God with our lives.

Many factors direct and influence our work behavior. At the most basic day-to-day level are customer expectations, instructions from the boss, and pressures at home. At the highest level is our desire to glorify God through our endeavors.

At the "macro" level is our universal need for significance, meaning, and purpose. Beyond this "big-picture, global" motivation, however, we each have a personal core motivation that will most strongly direct and control our work behavior.

Pyramid of Motivations

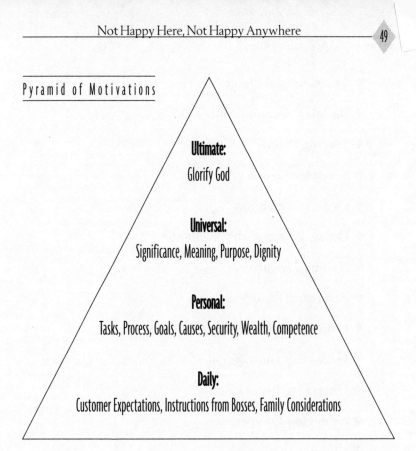

Ultimate:
Glorify God

Universal:
Significance, Meaning, Purpose, Dignity

Personal:
Tasks, Process, Goals, Causes, Security, Wealth, Competence

Daily:
Customer Expectations, Instructions from Bosses, Family Considerations

There are many personal core motivations. Here are the ones that occur to me. Can you think of others?

◆ **Accomplishing Tasks**

◆ **Participating in a Process**

◆ **Meeting Goals**

◆ **Solving Problems**

- ◆ **Creating Something**

- ◆ **Building Relationships**

- ◆ **Serving People**

- ◆ **Serving a Cause**

- ◆ **Organizing Things**

- ◆ **Doing Things with Excellence**

- ◆ **Building Security**

- ◆ **Acquiring Wealth**

- ◆ **Gaining Financial Independence**

- ◆ **Increasing Knowledge**

- ◆ **Observing Beauty**

- ◆ **Achieving Competence**

- ◆ **Other** _____

- ◆ **Other** _____

While all of these will motivate each of us to some extent, one or two will have primacy. Which ones animate you most? See if you can narrow it down to one or two.

For the first half of my career my core motivation was a "thing," an achievement, a quest, a goal to be accomplished. The stated overarching purpose of the company I used to own was "to acquire and develop 10,000,000 square feet of commercial real estate" by a certain date.

Can you see the problems with this purpose? It pinned my success to a future event over which I had limited control. It postponed my enjoyment to a much later date. It set me up to make unwise decisions just so I could keep making progress toward the goal.

Today my core motivation has changed to "service" — helping a customer, solving a problem, meeting a need. Perhaps it would have been better to state my former company's overarching purpose this way: "To acquire and develop commercial real estate that meets the growing demand of each market we serve."

To be truly happy depends in part on shifting from what we "get" out of our work to what we "give" to others through our work.

What if after all this — striking a right balance, coming to grips with not needing to know the future, and gaining understanding of your core motivation — you still don't like your job? Then go ahead and make a change.

A Guide to Changing Vocations

One day I was talking to a successful salesman, Eric, who was trying to decide whether to go into business for himself.

"If you are thinking of leaving your present employment, you really have two decisions to make," I suggested. "First, should you leave or stay? Second, if the decision is to leave, what should you do next?"

Eric had already made the first decision. Concerned about the unethical behavior he was observing in his boss, he wanted to get rid of the negative feelings that kept him awake at night. He had prayed a lot, sought much counsel, and waited patiently for a clear mind. He knew his decision had to be leaving. Now he was ready for the second step — what to do next.

I asked Eric, "In precise and exact language, what is the problem you're trying to solve?"

That's the first question to ask when changing companies or careers: *In precise and exact language, what is the problem you're trying to solve?* In my experience I have observed that too often we look for a solution without actually understanding the problem we're trying to solve.

For example, if you love your work but don't get along with your boss, the problem isn't merely "the need to change vocations," but something like "the need to find a place you can do the same work with a better employer." On the other hand, if you like your boss but don't love your work, your present boss may be able to help solve that problem by finding different work within your present organization. You may have to look at joining another employer, but not necessarily.

You can see the challenge. To look confidently *forward* to a good solution, you must look wisely *backward* to make sure you solve the *right* problem. It's crucial to solve the right problem.

Eric expounded on the problem he was trying to solve by saying, "I like the business field I'm in, but more than once I've gotten myself into a pickle by not asking more questions about the people I've worked for.

"I suppose my ultimate goal is financial independence. One thing that has slowed me down, though, is my aversion to risk.

"Also, I really want to spend *more* time with my family, not less. I know that the first few years of starting my own business would take more time. But I have a brother-in-law who started his own company five years ago and now he has a pretty flexible schedule."

As part of my follow-up I asked Eric these questions, which you may want to spend some time pondering as well.

- ◆ **What is the answer you want? What is the desire of your heart?**

- ◆ **What past tasks, roles, and responsibilities have you most enjoyed?**

- ◆ **When are you in your glory? What single thing most animates you?**

- ◆ **What does your wife say?**

◆ **What do your best friends say?**

◆ **How have you sensed God leading you?**

◆ **Do you have the passion to be an entrepreneur?**

◆ **How long would you be able to go without a paycheck?**

◆ **Would you need a financial partner? Do you have contacts for this?**

◆ **Are you trying to get away from a negative situation or move toward a positive situation?**

Here are some additional thoughts for men thinking about making a change:

Find that thing to do which, once discovered, you could be happy doing nothing else. Recheck the "Pyramid of Motivations" depicted earlier in this chapter. What is your core vocational motivation? Think first in terms of your "life work," and then look for a job where you can utilize your giftedness and demonstrate your motivated interest.

Half-listen to advice from friends. Listen carefully to friends, but always keep in mind: No one else can tell you what God's will is for your life. Personally I find that friends will often say, "Sounds great! Go ahead. You deserve it." In reality, they are often merely reflecting back to you that they think it's a romantic idea. They have not understood or cannot understand the many variables you must consider. Don't merely look for someone to ratify the decision you have already made.

Prioritize your work desires in relationship to other priorities. You may want to take on a bigger responsibility, enter an entirely different vocation, or start up your own company. However, it's important to see these desires in context. Weigh your desires in relationship to your family values, your financial goals, and the geographical area in which you want to live.

Analyze the new position before you take it, not after. Although there are exceptions, the best you will probably ever look to a potential employer is during your job interview. You, of course, want to put your best foot forward. Once you go to work, the warts start to show.

Conversely, the best a potential employer will probably ever look to you is also during your job interview. Like you, they also want to put their best foot forward. Eric mentioned that for his last two job changes he didn't do his homework. He more or less jumped into it. Be prepared to ask specific and direct questions, especially about those areas where you've experienced disappointment with previous employers.

Wait until the decision is clear. Wait until God "speaks" (or leads). If you have to ask whether or not he has spoken and you're hearing him clearly, he probably hasn't. Don't be in too much of a hurry. There are very few things in life that can't wait two weeks. God does not author confusion; Satan does. Peace should be your umpire, so wait until you sense it. If you don't wait for that peace to come upon you, you could be setting yourself up to make a huge mistake.

Self-Quiz for Making a Vocational Change

Are you thinking about making a vocational change? If so, here's a self-quiz to help you along the path:

- ◆ In precise and exact language, what is the problem you're trying to solve?

- ◆ First, should you leave or find a way to stay? Second, if the decision is to leave, what should you do next?

- ◆ What is the answer you want? What is the desire of your heart?

- ◆ What past tasks, roles, and responsibilities have you most enjoyed?

- ◆ When are you in your glory? What single thing most animates you?

◆ What is that thing to do which, once discovered, you could be happy doing nothing else?

◆ If married, what does your wife say?

◆ What do your best friends say?

◆ How have you sensed God leading you?

◆ Are you trying to get away from a negative situation or move toward a positive situation?

◆ Have you prioritized your work desires in relationship to other priorities?

◆ Have you analyzed the new position and organization carefully?

◆ Are you prepared to wait until the decision is clear?

For those considering starting up a business of your own, here are some additional questions:

◆ Do you have the passion to be an entrepreneur?

◆ How long would you be able to go without a paycheck?

◆ Would you need a financial partner? Do you have contacts for this?

Every man wants his work life to be meaningful and fulfilling. When we refrain from attaching too much of our identity to our work, balance our work responsibilities with our family responsibilities, enjoy the present process, understand our own motivated interests, and only make changes after careful thought, we will take a huge step toward becoming a happy man at work.

SECRET #3
VOCATION

Our core motivation as men is our desire to find significance, meaning, and dignity in who we are and what we do. Our vocations can help satisfy that desire, in large part, if we glorify God through our work by serving others. But a man who is unhappy in his work will find it difficult to be happy anywhere. For that reason, you should search for that occupation which, once discovered, you could be happy doing nothing else. At the same time, we must also remember that no amount of success at work can adequately compensate for failure at home.

FOCUS QUESTIONS

1. "When a man is unhappy in other areas of his life, he can still hold together a semblance of happiness. But he who is unhappy in his work is unhappy everywhere." Do you agree? How has this been true for you personally?

2. The two greatest areas in which we invest our time are family and work. How balanced have you been in these two priorities? What is one practical step you can take this week to bring them into better balance?

3. Do you tend to focus more on enjoying the "present process" or on "future accomplishment"? Why is focusing on what might happen in the future so frustrating? How could you lead a happier life by focusing more on the "process" than on the "future"?

4. Review the "Pyramid of Motivations." What is your personal core motivation? If you're not sure, review the list of choices on pages 49–50. Do you have the right ultimate motivation? If you don't, what should you do?

5. Are you happy in your work? If not, could you be happy where you are if certain things were reorganized? Whom would you speak to about it, and what would you say? If there is no way to be happy where you are, how would, or did, you answer the self-quiz questions in this chapter?

CHAPTER FOUR

STAGGERED BY THE ODD
GOODNESS OF GOD

STAGGERED BY THE ODD
GOODNESS OF GOD

My younger brother has endured a difficult twenty-year run of tragedy and disappointment.

The girl he loved married someone else, a crook stole his idea to start a business, his condominium burned down, his career got side-tracked, and, more recently, a few days after he purchased a used sport utility vehicle, the engine blew up—to mention only a few "highlights."

During the past two or three years he became depressed over the cumulative toll of all these and numerous other problems. So discouraged was he that when his condo unit was finally rebuilt he did nothing to redecorate and make it into a home.

One day he said, "What is God trying to tell me? What does he want me to do? If he would just tell me what it is, I'd do it."

The whole situation makes my heart ache. He's my brother, and I would do anything to help. And I've tried. But in the end it has been something he had to go through—something that *only* he could go through.

God hasn't yet answered my brother's questions, but recently some balance has begun to come back into his life. Not long ago we were riding together in the car when he said, "You know those pictures of the family I showed you the other day? Well, I bought some frames and I've started hanging them up. They really look good."

It was the first sign of hopefulness he had shown in many, many months. I knew then that he was going to be all right.

All Men Want to Be Happy

According to a report on the ABC Evening News, someone commits suicide in the United States every seventeen minutes.[1] You may be shocked to know that more people commit suicide than are murdered in the United States — 31,000 people. A staggering 500,000 additional people are treated in emergency rooms each year for attempted suicide.

Why do people take their own lives? Undoubtedly for a multitude of reasons — but at least for this reason: Because they think it will make them happy. The French scientist and religious philosopher Blaise Pascal said, "All men seek happiness. This is without exception. This is the motive of every action of every man, even those who hang themselves."

The Russian novelist Leo Tolstoy put it this way: "I believe the motive power of all our actions is personal happiness."

Whether you are fundamentally a happy man or not, one thing is certain: You are not always happy. In fact, the chief characteristic of a truly happy man is that he is not always happy.

Now why is that? Why are men not always happy?

---

1. Peter Jennings, *ABC Evening News* (Friday, July 17, 1998).

The Nature of Life

Life by its very nature contains the element of tragedy. Each day we are bumped, bruised, and scraped by sorrows, aches, pains, sufferings, trials, brokenness, heartaches—even despair and death. For many, life seems like a series of setbacks punctuated by occasional successes.

We are publicly embarrassed and privately confused by our sufferings because God promised peace and joy to his followers. Indeed, if the Christian life is one of joy and victory, most of the staff didn't get the memo.

In the movie *Patch Adams*, the lead character, Patch, played by Robin Williams, stands on a cliff and contemplates suicide after experiencing a bitter tragedy. He says, "God, I could throw myself off this cliff right now, and we both know that you wouldn't do anything to stop me." Then, after another moment of reflection, he says, "Ahh, you're not worth it," then turns and walks back to his car.

The "memo" that Patch missed—the one many of us didn't get—is that the world is not helpful. Not now, not ever. We live in a fallen world. We walk through our local mall past people with terminal diseases who don't even know yet that they have the disease, people addicted to drugs and alcohol, people battered by words or fists, greedy people who would figuratively slit your throat over a hundred dollars, wicked people who cheat and steal, and evil people who harm others physically, financially, emotionally, and psychologically.

Yet, God often gets blamed for the wrong or wicked things that happen to us. Or he gets blamed for the bad things we do to ourselves. Or for the bad things that "just happen," like my friend's wife and the mother of his four children who fell off a cliff to her death. Why did she fall? Because some loose rocks gave way as she stood on the edge.

God is not the problem, he is the solution to suffering and sorrow. The nature of life in this fallen world may be tragic, but the nature of God's kingdom is "righteousness, peace and joy in the Holy Spirit" (Romans 14:17).

Even so, a truly happy man has learned not to expect immunity from sorrow. In that light we must go on to ask the important question: How then do men suffer?

How Do Men Suffer?

There are very likely more ways to suffer than there are people to experience the suffering.

Suffering can come creeping in or crashing down. There are "windows" in our lives when circumstances creep up on us and get us down. Here are a few to consider. You can surely add your own experiences to the list:

◆ **demands of a young family**

◆ **marriage struggles**

◆ **pressures from work**

◆ **job dissatisfaction**

◆ **health problems**

◆ **too much month left at the end of the money**

◆ **crises of meaning**

◆ **identity confusion**

◆ **lack of purpose**

◆ **midlife experiences**

◆ **challenges of the empty-nest years**

◆ **stress-inducing events**

◆ **boredom**

There are still other windows of suffering, often more tragic, that open suddenly and unexpectedly:

- ◆ **A teenager breaks your heart**

- ◆ **A car strikes down a loved one**

- ◆ **Your home is burglarized or your car is stolen**

- ◆ **Your finances undergo a sudden reversal**

- ◆ **Your wife says she wants a divorce**

- ◆ **You have a moral failure**

- ◆ **You suffer a heart attack or stroke**

- ◆ **You are diagnosed with cancer**

The big three windows of suffering for most men, though, can be located in three key areas:

- ◆ **marriage**

- ◆ **money**

- ◆ **meaning**

Perhaps the time has come to ask this very personal question: How have *you* been suffering in your life recently?

Sometimes these windows of suffering become too much for us to handle, and we experience a myriad of feelings. At one time or another we may feel...

- ◆ **lonely**

- ◆ **isolated**

- ◆ **empty**

- ◆ **overwhelmed**

- ◆ **weary**

- ◆ **disappointed**

- ◆ **disillusioned**

- ◆ **guilty**

- ◆ **frustrated**

- ◆ **confused**

- ◆ **angry**

- ◆ **bitter**

- ◆ **resentful**

- ◆ **fearful**

Have you experienced any of these feelings in recent days and weeks? Can you pinpoint why you have these feelings? Having reflected on the question of how men suffer, it's good to pose another vital question: Why then do men suffer?

Why Do Men Suffer?

While the ways we suffer are myriad, the reasons we suffer are relatively few.

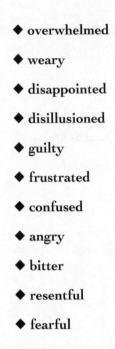

Suffering is a vocation. Suffering is "part" of what it means to be a Christian. Part of the "vocation," or calling, of a Christian is to suffer.

To suffer is human; to suffer with a purpose is Christian. Suffering is, quite frankly, part of "the order of things." When the apostles of the early church were flogged, they left "rejoicing because they had been counted worthy of suffering disgrace for the Name" (Acts 5:41).

The apostle Paul and his associate Barnabas taught the followers of Jesus, "We must go through many hardships to enter the kingdom of God" (Acts 14:22). Elsewhere Paul wrote, "For it has been granted to you on behalf of Christ not only to believe on him, but also to suffer for him" (Philippians 1:29).

Suffering isn't necessarily related to your behavior. Ironically, you don't have to do something wrong to suffer. You will, of course, suffer for doing wrong, but also for doing right. The apostle Peter wrote,

> *Dear friends, do not be surprised at the painful trial you are suffering, as though something strange were happening to you. But rejoice that you participate in the sufferings of Christ, so that you may be overjoyed when his glory is revealed. If you are insulted because of the name of Christ, you are blessed, for the Spirit of glory and of God rests on you. If you suffer, it should not be as a murderer or thief or any other kind of criminal, or even as a meddler. However, if you suffer as a Christian, do not be ashamed, but praise God that you bear that name.*
>
> I PETER 4:12–16

Suffering can be for discipline. One of the ways God chooses to shape our character is to discipline us, which has the natural side effect that it hurts. "'The Lord disciplines those he loves, and he punishes everyone he accepts as a son.' Endure hardship as discipline; God is treating you as sons. For what son is not disciplined by his father?" (Hebrews 12:6–7). Ponder this example of suffering as discipline: A man allowed his overly busy work schedule to squeeze the emotional love out of his marriage. As a plea for help, his wife asked him for a trial separation. God used those months to get his attention and to begin a process of real change in his life. Tragedies are not good, but they do have the potential to turn our hearts toward God.

Suffering can lead to salvation. One evening a man named Mike, childless for a number of years, not a believer in Jesus, watched a television program about children with special needs. Later that evening, while on a walk through the neighborhood with his wife, his thoughts turned to the television program, and he said to his wife, "We could handle that."

Two years later their first child was born, a son. He came into the world with the congenital condition known as Down's syndrome. Some time later, Mike expressed his honest emotions regarding what had been happening in his life: "It was unbelievably hard at first. Three years later, I couldn't handle it anymore. I cried out to God, and I gave my life to Jesus Christ."

Is being the father of a son with Down's syndrome an experience of suffering? Absolutely. Can that kind of suffering seem futile? Of course. Is it bad news? Who are we to say?

A man is happy not because he suffers, but because he understands, by faith, that God can, and does, use suffering for good.

The apostle Paul wrote, "The creation was subjected to frustration [synonyms: futility, meaninglessness, vanity], not by its own choice, but by the will of the one who subjected it [that is, by the will of God] ..."

Why on earth would God do *that?* "... in hope that the creation itself will be liberated from its bondage to decay and brought into the glorious freedom of the children of God" (Romans 8:20–21).

Because God desires for men to be part of "his forever family," he makes every worldly pursuit lead ultimately to futility and frustration. Why? Because God knows that if you and I could find purpose and meaning in any worldly pursuit apart from him, we would surely pursue it.

So God makes every avenue that leads away from him into a dead end. Apart from him life has no meaning. Read carefully the next sentence, which asserts that God is sovereign while preserving the free will of human beings: Futility is the chief tool God uses to sovereignly draw men to himself of their own free will. In other words, God turns up the heat until we freely choose to leave the devil's kitchen.

Suffering can be for equipping. Sometimes we feel pain from the hand of God because he wants to make us more fruitful in serving him.

In John 15, Jesus uses the analogy that he is the true vine and the Father is the gardener. He says, "He [the Father] cuts off every branch in me that bears no fruit" (John 15:2a). This is a stern warning to unbelievers.

But then he says the most amazing thing: "While every branch that *does* bear fruit [in other words, believers] *he prunes* so that it will be even more fruitful" (John 15:2b, italics added). Remarkable! Basically, whether you believe or whether you don't — you're going to get cut. I'll bet nobody told you *that* when they asked you if you wanted to give your life to Jesus!

Consider the story of Art and his wife, who fought all the way to a marriage conference at which I was teaching. "I'm having a crisis of faith," said Art. "I feel abandoned by God. I'm depressed and mopey. I can't sleep. I just can't understand how or why God would allow two people like us, people who have professed faith in Jesus, people who are committed Christians, to be at each other's throats like this."

I suggested to Art, "Often what we view as abandonment is really what should be seen as equipping. God wants to work certain qualities of character into our lives, while 'pruning' other qualities. There can be no doubt that God is interested in the success of our circumstances: 'For I know the plans I have for you, declares the LORD, plans to prosper you and not to harm you' (Jeremiah 29:11). However, God will not hesitate to blow up our circumstances to get at our character. That's because he's far more interested in what 'kind' of men we become than what we have when we get there.

"Right now you both are focused on each other's problems and absorbed with satisfying your own needs and demanding your own rights. God wants to take what you view as abandonment and use it to equip you to be a better husband. Why not dwell on that? Why not take some time to concentrate on serving her instead of changing or controlling her."

Suffering is worth the price. The Bible is unmistakably clear: "I consider that our present sufferings are not worth comparing with the glory that will be revealed in us" (Romans 8:18).

The Odd Goodness of God

David and I first met when he was the chief taskmaster putting together a men's event where I spoke. Incredibly successful in business, he possessed administrative skills and a bubbly personality that pushed the event over the top—it was wildly successful.

One day he told me, "When I began my career I turned my back on God for seventeen years. I took credit for all my success. But then God took everything away. My success. My wife. Even my children. That got my attention. In a strange way, it was good that I failed. Now I'm rebuilding, but with a whole different perspective. It looks like I might even be given the opportunity to restore my marriage."

Like this David, the biblical King David saw an odd goodness to his sufferings. He said, "The suffering you sent was good for me, for it taught me to pay attention to your principles" (Psalm 119:71, NEW LIVING TRANSLATION).

Consider too the story of John, a bank vice president who finds no pleasure in the job that once animated him. His boss has lost confidence in him and is constantly on his case. Yet every door he has tried to open while looking for something new has been locked.

Wisely, he said, "I guess this is something I'm just going to have to go through. That great Old Testament man named Joseph spent many years living in adversity. Yet God had a plan for his life. What some intended for evil, God used for good. So I've decided to just take my time and enjoy this. I'm going to let God remove whatever he wants to remove from my life, and I'll trust him to remake me into a better man." John has discovered the odd goodness of God.

And then there was Marcus. When Marcus was forty-eight years old, a car full of drunk teenagers ran a stop sign, smashed into the car in which his own teenage son Kenny was riding, and Kenny's life was snuffed out.

Ironically, this tragedy happened on Good Friday. Marcus experienced that day something of what Jesus' mother must have felt as she stood at the foot of the cross and watched her precious son suffer indescribable pain and then take his final breath on earth.

Marcus and his other son wanted revenge. They took the boys to court, but justice eluded them. Nobody served any prison time for causing Kenny's death.

Two years went by, and the stress of the unresolved pain and sorrow began to take its toll. One day Marcus was taken to the hospital, where surgeons connected four bypasses around his heart. Later he said, "I was afraid I was going to die. But the surgery was successful. On top of that, since my surgery I've had two angioplasty procedures. At this point, I'm not afraid of anything.

"Through all this, I have made peace with God, and my bitterness over Kenny's death has gone away. You know, there are things to remember and things to forget. My bitterness over Kenny's death is something to forget. I just wish my other son could let it go. For him, it has become the thing to remember."

Part of the odd goodness of God is that he doesn't prevent seemingly random sufferings from afflicting us, but he does ease our pain—if we will let him. It is both odd that we must suffer at all and good that we are not left in bondage to despair forever. During the suffering of Job one of his friends said, "But by means of their suffering, [God] rescues those who suffer. For he gets their attention through adversity" (Job 36:15, NEW LIVING TRANSLATION).

Finally, the story of Justin gives us hope in the ultimate goodness of God. Just as his real estate development business was finally hitting stride, Justin and his wife found out that she had a serious, often terminal type of cancer. As a result, he completely reordered his priorities to spend more time with her.

Later Justin shared this: "You know, God has done a remarkable thing. My business is far more successful than it ever was before, now that I'm spending less time worrying about it." Part of the odd goodness of God is that while we suffer in one area, he often takes up the slack for us in another area.

God can take care of you if you will trust him. He is more than able to meet your needs. In light of Justin's story, here's a great question to ask yourself if you're married: What would you begin doing differently today if you learned your wife had cancer? You may want to begin doing that very thing right now.

Take some time right now to name your sufferings, sorrows, trials, temptations, tragedies, frustrations, futilities, prunings, and heartaches. Why do you think God has allowed them?

SECRET #4
SUFFERING

An old black woman in the Deep South put suffering in proper perspective when she said, "If the mountain was smooth, you couldn't climb it." Everything God has caused or allowed in your life is for your good — to draw you into a deeper love relationship with him. Your sufferings are not merely setbacks. They are also springboards to the crucial task of knowing God well enough that you can trust him. We must learn to interpret the mysteries of life in the light of our knowledge of God. Until we can look the darkest fact full in the face without damaging God's character, we do not yet know him as he is.

Still Suffering

On a sunny day years ago the great preacher Donald Barnhouse and his children were driving to a cemetery to bury his wife and their mother. At a traffic light a semi-tractor trailer pulled up beside them, casting its shadow on them and blocking the sunlight.

Barnhouse said to his children, "That's what's happened to us. We have been hit by the shadow, but not by the truck."

If you are in the middle of a season of suffering, consider these words of encouragement from one who knew suffering better than most, a first-century man by the name of Paul, whose words have been preserved for all time for our comfort and edification:

> *Therefore we do not lose heart. Though outwardly we are wasting away, yet inwardly we are being renewed day by day. For our light and momentary troubles are achieving for us an eternal glory that far outweighs them all. So we fix our eyes not on what is seen, but on what is unseen. For what is seen is temporary, but what is unseen is eternal.*
>
> 2 CORINTHIANS 4:16–18

If you know Jesus Christ, and still you are all too familiar with suffering, take comfort. Do not lose heart, for you have been "hit by the shadow, but not by the truck."

FOCUS QUESTIONS

1. What has been the happiest season of your life, and what made it that way?

2. How do you suffer? How have you understood suffering — as a thing to be avoided at all costs, as punishment, as a random occurrence, or in some other way?

3. Looking back at the section "Why Do Men Suffer?" how can you see God working in your life in these ways?

4. Can you describe a time of suffering or futility in your life when you sensed "the odd goodness of God"?

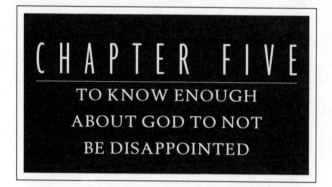

CHAPTER FIVE

TO KNOW ENOUGH
ABOUT GOD TO NOT
BE DISAPPOINTED

To Know Enough About God to Not Be Disappointed

One day my son, a shooting guard on his Christian high school team, was playing in a basketball game at the gym of a longtime rival—also a Christian high school. Some of our fans were getting a little too animated, a bit too much "into" the game.

Finally, the referee stopped in front of our section in the stands and yelled out, "You're Christians! Act like it!" Admittedly a bit unusual, but it raises a good question. How does a Christian know how to act?

The Two Problems

There are two significant problems that keep men from enjoying a happy life in fellowship with Jesus Christ.

First, most men only know enough about God to be disappointed with him. They listen to the sermons, they try to do the right things, they have it in their hearts to be faithful Christians, but they don't seem to possess much joy, and they certainly seem to lack consistent victory over sinful habits. Often they feel a nagging sense of shame. Why?

Perhaps for several reasons, but at least for many it's because they have never actually been "educated" about what it means to "be" Christian. They are not disciples.

Many of us tend to think, "Well, I've learned about Jesus. Now it's time to move on to the next thing." Like politicians working a crowd, we meet Jesus, then move on to the next interesting idea about how to improve our lives. We never actually devote the time to grow into an intimate friendship with and a life-changing knowledge of God.

Second, most churches are not making disciples. We have a great problem in the church today. An executive in a major denomination acknowledged one day in a moment of courageous candor, "Our churches are not making disciples." But that's not the real problem. The real problem is—*our churches think they are.*

The list of problems that plague the church is virtually endless. And yet, the church is the single best hope of this present civilization. It's important to state that just because the church is part of the problem doesn't mean it can't be part of the solution. For men to experience any degree of progress in spiritual maturity the church must humbly and obediently return to its mission of making disciples. In his great commission to his followers (Matthew 28:19-20), Jesus didn't say, "Therefore, go and make Presbyterians (or Baptists or Methodists) of all nations ..." He didn't say make churches, or workers, or tithers. He said, "Make *disciples...*"

To be truly happy a man must become a disciple, and it is the mission of the church to make disciples. In this chapter we'll investigate the answers to questions like these: Why do you need to be a disciple? What does it mean to be a disciple? And how do you go about living like a disciple?

Why You Need to Be a Disciple

Whether they realize it or not, men have a desperate need to be encouraged. Encouragement is the food of the heart, and every heart is a hungry heart. Today our churches are filled with men who have broken wings. The church needs to be a hospital to love, "doctor," and heal them.

However, it can't stop there. Once a certain point of stability and maturity is reached we need to shift from *healing* to *building up* in spiritual knowledge. Perhaps nothing is more encouraging than knowledge—knowing why, what, and how—why things are the way they are, what to do in the situations of life, and how to do it. The single best way to encourage a man long term is to train him to be a disciple. Here's a simple suggestion for a credo for the church today: Love your weak men, but disciple the strong.

Most men have it in their hearts to do the right thing. What's often missing is to know enough about God so they know what the right thing is.

Why don't more men become disciples? We can learn something from the dad who approached the coach of his son's high school soccer team and said, "My son doesn't know what the purpose of soccer is. He thinks it's to win a state championship. He has no idea of what you're trying to build into his life. Will you talk to him?"

Often men don't become disciples because they don't understand what the purpose of discipleship is. They've heard *that* they need to become disciples, but no one bothered to tell them *why*. They feel no sense of urgency or gravity to becoming a disciple.

Here's why they need to become a disciple. Passing the bar exam will give you a ticket to practice law, but it won't make you a good lawyer. In a similar way, becoming a *believer* will give you a ticket to heaven, but it won't make you a good Christian. For that you must become a *disciple*. To experience the deep joy of your faith and the abundant life offered through Jesus you must become a disciple.

What It Means to Be a Disciple

Can you define what it means to be a disciple?

Frequently men hear the term *disciple* but don't know exactly what it means, and often they're so established in their church that they're too embarrassed to ask.

So what *does* it mean to be a disciple?

SECRET #5
DISCIPLESHIP

Most of us have heard someone say (or maybe we've said it ourselves), "I knew *about* God, but I didn't know *God.*" Perhaps a greater problem today is that men do know God, but they don't know about him. To know God is to be a Christian. To know about God, however, is what it means to become a disciple.

The simple meaning of the term *disciple* in Jesus' day was "the pupil of a teacher." When used to describe a Christian, though, the term can be expanded to also mean "a follower" of Jesus, and an "adherent" to his teaching. A disciple has a *personal allegiance* to his teacher, Jesus. The life of a disciple revolves around Christ.

Take some time to reflect on this working definition of what it means to be a disciple: *A disciple is one called to walk with Christ, equipped to live like Christ, and sent to work for Christ.* Now let's take a look at how this process of calling, equipping, and sending works.

Calling, Equipping, Sending

God "called" the prophet Isaiah by revealing his glory so profoundly that Isaiah responded in repentance, "Woe to me! ... I am ruined! For I am a man of unclean lips" (Isaiah 6:5).

At this expression of repentance, God sent a spiritual being with a hot coal to touch Isaiah's lips, and the seraph said, "See, this has touched your lips; your guilt is taken away and your sin atoned for" (Isaiah 6:7). The first "calling" of God is to salvation.

Some time later God *sent* Isaiah. Isaiah recorded it this way: "Then I heard the voice of the Lord saying, 'Whom shall I send? And who will go for us?' And I said, 'Here am I. Send me!'" (Isaiah 6:8). I say "some time later God sent Isaiah," because Isaiah would not soon have been able to speak after a hot coal seared his lips. Lips are one of the most sensitive parts of the body. What happened during Isaiah's recuperation period? While we can't say for sure, this undoubtedly must have been the time God "equipped" Isaiah for what lay ahead.

There you have it! Calling, equipping, and sending. It's the "process" of becoming a disciple.

It was the experience of the apostle Paul—called on the Damascus road, then brought to Arabia and Tarsus to be equipped, then sent to the Greek-speaking world to proclaim the gospel.

It was the experience of the shepherd boy David—called to be the king, hounded by Saul for over a decade while in the process of being equipped, then sent to take the throne as king over all Israel.

It was the experience of the patriarch Jacob's favorite son Joseph—called to rule over his brothers, sold into Egypt for a time of equipping, then sent to rule Egypt and to save his family from famine.

It was the experience of Moses—called to be the deliverer of his people the Israelites, driven into the desert for forty years of equipping, then sent to lead his people out of Egypt.

Let's take a closer look at how the process of calling, equipping, and sending applies to you and me—disciples in the making.

CALLED

A disciple is called to walk with Christ.

At sunrise one morning I was stretching out after returning from a vigorous row in my one-man scull. A formation of six mallard ducks soared back and forth in front of me several times, then skidded across the water and came to a halt a few yards in front of me. Lamenting the fact that my wife had not seen this mini-drama, I thought, "This is a great show, but you can't enjoy it unless you're in the theater!"

In much the same way, the beauty, perfections, character, and attributes of God can only be observed if we answer the call to be where he is—you have to purchase your ticket, go into the theater, and be "with him." It would be absurd to go to a theater, say hello to the ticket clerk, then skip watching the movie so you could sit in a coffee shop and discuss the movie with friends.

To be a disciple means to be "with Christ." Jesus used a fascinating approach to change men. He never scolded them, "You're Christians! Act like it!" Instead, he invited men to come and be "with him" (Mark 3:13–14). Jesus issues the invitation to all men to "come, follow me" (Mark 1:17).

It was a strategy that worked. One day not long after Jesus died, during the course of boldly proclaiming the gospel message, the disciples Peter and John were arrested and brought to trial. The Bible says, "When they [members of the Sanhedrin] saw the courage of Peter and John and realized that they were unschooled, ordinary men, they were astonished and they took note that these men had been *with Jesus*" (Acts 4:13, italics added).

EQUIPPED

A disciple is equipped to live like Christ.

If you've ever had braces attached to your teeth, you know that after a brief adjustment period you don't notice them. Yet they're always there, applying steady, constant pressure. And over a long period of time, they change the location of your teeth. That's a lot like how we are equipped to live like Christ.

Discipleship means to "attach" Jesus to our minds and hearts. It means to let him apply the gentle, steady, constant pressure that will change the location of our desires, motivations, and ambitions. It's a slow process. To become a disciple means entering into a long-term process to increasingly become more like Jesus.

When your teeth finally straightened out and the orthodontist removed the braces, do you remember what he warned would happen if you didn't wear your retainer every night? He said your teeth would go back to their old location! In much the same way, there is never a time when we no longer need to be equipped. In fact, the more we do as "sent" men, the more we need the encouragement of continual equipping. We each need to be in a Bible study or small group where we can continue to grow and be encouraged.

When a man takes time to be "with Jesus," what will he learn? The disciples who sat at Jesus' feet learned what it meant to love, pray, worship, serve, cry, obey, humble themselves, be under authority, resolve conflict, take care of the poor, resist evil, denounce hypocrisy, and have compassion—all in the very way Jesus did those things.

Today we can't *literally* be "with Jesus" in order to be equipped, yet through the Scriptures his life and teachings can spring to life and profoundly shape us. We are equipped by means of the Bible: "All Scripture is God-breathed and is useful for teaching, rebuking, correcting and training in righteousness, *so that the man of God may be thoroughly equipped* for every good work" (2 Timothy 3:16–17, italics added).

SENT

A disciple is sent to work for Christ.

Why does Jesus want to equip us? The *activity* of equipping is to teach us, rebuke us, correct us, and train us in righteousness. Notice in the passage from 2 Timothy 3:16–17, however, the *purpose* of equipping: "so that the man of God may be thoroughly equipped *for every good work*" (italics added).

Calling is for our salvation, while equipping is for our sending. Jesus puts his men to work. Jesus prayed, "As you sent me into the world, I have sent them into the world" (John 17:18). He says to us, "This is to my Father's glory, that you *bear much fruit,* showing yourselves to be *my disciples*" (John 15:8, italics added).

Jesus does not send us out ill-equipped. Neither does he send us alone. Consider this analogy from the world of auto racing. Because of

NASCAR racing aerodynamics, two cars drafting each other can go faster than one can go alone. The headwinds buffet and bounce the lead car around. However, if you're drafting behind the leader you actually have to take your foot off the accelerator a bit. The lead car actually pulls you along.

When we draft behind Jesus we can do more than we could ever do alone. He will take the headwinds on our behalf. We can take our foot off the accelerator. He will pull us along. That's what it means to be sent to work for Christ. Let's not try to go it alone. Let's not try to get out in front of him. But let's not lag behind him either, or we'll lose the benefit of his draft.

How You Can Live Like a Disciple – an Action Plan

What if you have had a genuine "born again" experience but you are not as fruitful as you would like to be? How can you become a more fruitful disciple? Consider these few suggestions. And while you're at it, why not write down specific, practical steps you would like to take as a result of reading these suggestions.

First, decide if you really want to be a better disciple. It is a good thing for a man to decide in advance how much he is willing to be changed. Are you serious about becoming a true disciple? Is that what you really want?

Let's consider the price. The great German theologian Dietrich Bonhoeffer said in his gem, *The Cost of Discipleship,* "When Christ calls a man he bids him come and die." Bonhoeffer despised cheap grace, which he defined as the preaching of forgiveness without requiring repentance, baptism without church discipline, communion without confession, grace without discipleship, grace without the cross, and grace without the living, incarnate Jesus Christ.[1]

---

1. Dietrich Bonhoeffer, *The Cost of Discipleship* (New York: Collier Books, 1963), 47.

Bonhoeffer went on to offer these profound thoughts about genuine grace:

> Costly grace is the gospel which must be sought again and again, the gift which must be asked for, the door at which a man must knock. Such grace is costly because it calls us to follow, and it is grace because it calls us to follow Jesus Christ. It is costly because it costs a man his life, and it is grace because it gives a man the only true life. It is costly because it condemns sin, and grace because it justifies the sinner. Above all, it is costly because it cost God the life of his Son: 'we were bought at a price,' and what has cost God much cannot be cheap for us. Above all, it is grace because God did not reckon his Son too dear a price to pay for our life, but delivered him up for us. Costly grace is the Incarnation of God.[2] [emphasis added]

For Bonhoeffer, there is little value in talking about a relationship with Jesus Christ apart from obedience. For him, obedience is the meaning of discipleship. He wants his reader to see that Jesus Christ makes a radical call on the life of the believer—a call to follow Jesus, which is demonstrated by obedience.

The life of discipleship is that narrow road of obedience, self-sacrifice, and self-denial that leads to the broad road of joy, peace, and happiness. Jesus said it is the only way: "If anyone would come after me, he must deny himself and take up his cross daily and follow me" (Luke 9:23). Jesus also said, "In the same way, any of you who does not give up everything he has cannot be my disciple" (Luke 14:33).

So how can you become a better disciple? The answer in two words: Be obedient.

Second, learn to "abide" in Christ. Jesus said, "If a man remains [abides] in me and I in him, he will bear much fruit" (John 15:5).

---

2. Bonhoeffer, *The Cost of Discipleship*, 48–49.

It's hard to not get distracted by distractions. That's why they call them distractions. To become a disciple means giving up all distractions that keep us from making Jesus first in our lives. Søren Kierkegaard, in his book *Purity of Heart Is To Will One Thing,* says that the grave danger for us is that we become double-minded (James 1:5—8). How important it is for us to be aware of our own motivations! We become double-minded when we want to be a disciple...

♦ **for the sake of the reward — what we can get out of it,**

♦ **out of fear of punishment — what will happen to us if we don't, or**

♦ **only up to a certain degree — an unwillingness to fully commit ourselves.**

To abide in Christ is to live wholeheartedly for him. Unfortunately, when we ask men to live all out for Jesus Christ, it sometimes sounds like we're asking them to work hard for God's approval—"perform and get a reward." Exactly not that. Popular author Jerry Bridges knew what it was like to fall victim to that way of thinking. At the beginning of his walk with Christ, he was given *The Seven Spiritual Disciplines,* published by The Navigators. He wasn't told he would earn favor with God by doing these spiritual disciplines, nor was he told that he would lose God's blessing if he didn't do them, but he assumed it. Our faith and hope is in Jesus Christ—abiding in him—not in the "activity" we choose to know him better.

Third, don't hold so tightly to the idea of a "quiet time." Where did the idea of a quiet time come from? The Bible counsels us to pray continually (1 Thessalonians 5:17) and to pray in the Spirit on all occasions (Ephesians 6:18), and it reminds us that he who meditates on God's Word day and night will prosper in everything he does (Psalm 1:2—3). Why turn off the faucet just when the hot water finally makes its way through the pipes? Sure, it's great to reserve a "quiet time" for Bible reading and prayer (I wouldn't be willing to give mine up), but we need to move on from there to a continual fellowship with Jesus Christ throughout the day. Make your quiet time a "special" time with God, but not your "only" time. Brother Lawrence wrote in *The Practice of the Presence of God,* "I have quitted all forms of devotion and set prayers but those to which my state obliges me. And I make it my business only to persevere in His holy presence."

Fourth, live by the pledge of a clean heart and conscience. My son has committed himself to a clean walk with God. One day when he was a senior in high school, someone returned the Snoop Doggy Dog CD he had borrowed from my son a couple of years earlier. He popped it into his car player a couple of times and listened. A few days later he ejected the CD, rolled down the window, and tossed it out like a Frisbee. When he told me what he had done, I asked him, "Why did you do that?"

He said, "Dad, I have a very strong Christian worldview. I am able to distinguish between what's right and wrong without getting confused. But the lyrics on that CD contain a lot of cuss words. I found they were getting 'stuck' in my mind. So I decided to get rid of it."

As only the apostle Paul could put it, "In a wealthy home some utensils are made of gold and silver, and some are made of wood and clay. The expensive utensils are used for special occasions, and the cheap ones are for everyday use. If you keep yourself pure, you will be a utensil God can use for his purpose. Your life will be clean, and you will be ready for the Master to use you for every good work" (2 Timothy 2:20–21, NEW LIVING TRANSLATION).

FOCUS QUESTIONS

1. **"Most men only know enough about God to be disappointed with him." Do you agree or do you disagree, and why? What are some of the things that can happen when a man doesn't really know *about* God?**

2. Is your church, if you belong to one, making disciples? Why is it important to be a disciple? Why is it important to be a part of a church fellowship?

3. In this chapter a working definition of a disciple was offered: *A disciple is one called to walk with Christ, equipped to live like Christ, and sent to work for Christ.* Are you being equipped to live like Christ? If so, how? If not, what is one practical step you can take this week to begin becoming equipped? Have you been sent to work for Christ? How? If you haven't been sent, what is one practical step you can take this week to live as a "sent" man?

4. Do you really want to be a better disciple? If so, how much are you willing to be changed? Is there some area of your life in which you have been disobedient to Christ? If so, are you willing to become obedient?

5. What does it mean to "abide in Christ"? What is one step you can take to more firmly abide in Christ in the coming week?

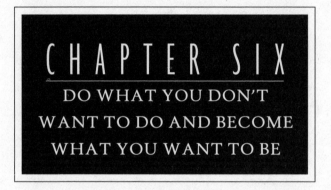

CHAPTER SIX

DO WHAT YOU DON'T WANT TO DO AND BECOME WHAT YOU WANT TO BE

6

DO WHAT YOU DON'T WANT TO DO AND BECOME WHAT YOU WANT TO BE

A while back a man named Randy took an exciting, high-income job that sent him around the world. Two years later he suffered from fatigue, stress, family strains, and emotional exhaustion. His friends have offered to do anything they could to help, but only Randy can put his life back on an even keel.

If your health fails, your marriage hits the rocks, or your finances reverse, people will feel sorry for you, but they won't feel responsible. Why not? Because you're the one who has to take responsibility for your own life.

In the first part of this chapter we will explore how we should "approach" responsibility for our lives. Then we'll conclude by taking a look at the realms of money, possessions, family, rest, and health. We'll discover that if you will do what you don't want to do, you will become what you want to be.

If God Is Sovereign, Why Pray?

We are responsible for our lives. That fact is at the core of the concept called stewardship. But God is sovereign. How can we be responsible for that over which God is sovereign?

When a large business deal I had worked on for six months looked like it was going to fall through, I asked my wife and son to pray about it with me.

When it was my turn to pray, I essentially begged God to let the deal go through, then concluded, "God, you already know what's going to happen. In fact, you have sovereignly decided what is the pleasure of your will. Give us wisdom to not miss the way."

When I finished, my son asked, "Dad, if God has already decided what's going to happen, why pray?" What a great question!

God is sovereign, but we are also responsible. The Scriptures place these two ideas side by side, without apology and without much explanation. In fact, we see this principle throughout the Bible. Here are a few examples. You undoubtedly could add others:

♦ "In his heart a man plans his course [our responsibility], but the LORD determines his steps [God's sovereignty]" (Proverbs 16:9).

♦ "The horse is made ready for the day of battle [our responsibility], but victory rests with the LORD [God's sovereignty]" (Proverbs 21:31).

♦ "Unless the LORD builds the house [God's sovereignty], its builders labor [our responsibility] in vain" (Psalm 127:1).

♦ David wrote, "I do not trust in my bow, my sword does not bring me victory; but you give us victory over our enemies" (Psalm 44:6). David didn't trust in his bow, but in God. But neither did he throw his bow away. He used it with all the skill he could muster.

◆ Paul wrote, "To this end I labor [our responsibility], struggling with all his energy, which so powerfully works in me [God's sovereignty]" (Colossians 1:29).

◆ Paul wrote, "I planted the seed, Apollos watered it [our responsibility], but God made it grow [God's sovereignty]" (1 Corinthians 3:6).

On top of all this, God invites, even instructs, us to "pray in the Spirit on all occasions with all kinds of prayers and requests" (Ephesians 6:18).

This truth that "God is sovereign, but we are responsible" lies at the heart of stewardship. At its core, stewardship means receiving all our abilities, resources, love, relationships, spiritual gifts, possessions, and places as "gifts on loan" from a sovereign God. It means that we maintain an attitude of accountable responsibility tempered by profound gratitude.

As stewards, we don't control how our circumstances will turn out. As stewards, we can't predict success. Nehemiah (in the Bible book called by his name) didn't know what would happen when Tobiah and Sanballat announced a plot to keep him from rebuilding the Jerusalem wall. So Nehemiah said, "We prayed to our God and posted a guard day and night to meet this threat" (Nehemiah 4:9). In other words, he trusted God and took responsibility to do what he could. It's sort of like the old saying, "Praise the Lord and pass the ammunition!" The famous nineteenth-century evangelist D. L. Moody put it this way, "We pray like it is all up to God, but we work like it is all up to us."

Therefore, our part is to be faithful, and God's part is to do whatever he deems best because he's God. So go back with me to the question posed by my son: Why pray? I hoped that my son would understand "our part" is to pray, because we can trust God to always work the "best" answer out. He did understand, and he felt good about it. Sure enough, a couple of weeks later, after a few adjustments, my business deal closed.

We are responsible to faithfully manage whatever God entrusts to our care. Stewardship is our responsibility to be faithful, not as *owners* (for God owns all things), but as *managers*.

Consider these differences in attitude between a steward and a non-steward:

Stewards "Know" . . .	Non-Stewards "Think" . . .
I am a manager	I am the owner
To be responsible is to be faithful	To be responsible I need control
I will be happy with what I get	I will be happy if I get what I want
Life is a process	All that counts is how it ends
I will be happy in the present	I need to worry about the future
My motive is gratitude	My motive is duty
God produces fruit through me	I must produce fruit to please God

Giving God the Last Word

For the first twenty years of our marriage I talked at least weekly about moving to a lakefront home. Nearly every week I would scout around for the latest properties on the market.

In the meantime, our daughter grew up and left for college. A year later, when our son was a sophomore in high school, my wife Patsy said one day, "Why don't we just forget the idea of moving to a lake until John goes to college. The home we have is so convenient to the school.

After that, we can move anywhere in the world and it won't make any difference." We talked it over for a few more minutes, and I agreed. It made perfectly good sense. In fact, I thought we had put it to rest once and for all.

Three days later I was driving from an appointment and saw a new "For Sale" sign that announced the availability of a lakefront lot at the end of a dirt road. Out of habit I turned off the main road and drove to a lovely spot. As nice as it was, I knew we had just decided to wait, so I dismissed it from my mind and drove on.

That night we attended a dinner party and on the way home passed near the dirt road with the lot. Again, purely out of habit, even though it was 11:00 P.M. I decided to show the lot to my wife. Patsy is the poster child for slow, deliberate, considered decision making. Little did I suspect what was about to take place. As we pulled onto the lot and eased down to the water's edge, Patsy blurted out, "Let's buy this lot."

Well, after picking myself up off the floor of the car, I said, "Patsy, I didn't bring you here to try and sell you on buying a lot. Three days ago we gave this idea up."

She said, "I know, but let's buy it anyway."

I said, "You're crazy, but let's pray about it, and, if we sense the Lord might be in this, I'll call the owner tomorrow. They'll probably want a fortune for it anyway."

We prayed. The next morning I called the owner. When he told me his asking price, I almost swallowed my tongue. It was extremely low. "What's wrong with this lot? Why are you selling it?" I asked.

He explained, "Well, I found a lot on a point of land with water on three sides further down the lake, so I need to sell this lot in order to close on the other." He met us at the property later that morning and, after some discussion, it was clear he was willing to offer a steep discount for a quick closing. We made an offer to close in two weeks and shook hands on what I considered to be a very good price.

Later that day the seller called. "We have a problem," he began awkwardly. "Before we met I put a call in to a guy who had told me to let him know if I ever wanted to sell. After I got home from meeting you, he called and he's willing to pay $10,000 more for the lot."

I've been around the block at least twice. This wasn't the first time a phantom "other buyer" had appeared on a deal in which I was interested. I said, "So."

"Well, I wanted to give you the right of first refusal since we had met on it this morning," he said.

"First refusal on what?" I asked.

"You know, to match his offer."

"I'm not sure what you're getting at," I replied. "Did we shake hands and make a deal this morning or not?"

"Well, yes, but we haven't signed a contract yet," he said. "And that was before this other fellow offered $10,000 more."

My mind went back over twenty years of searching for a lakefront property. We had always tried to be good stewards of God's resources. This decision had seemed right to us after earnestly seeking God's counsel in prayer, especially under the bizarre circumstances in which we found the lot and made the offer. But, I thought to myself, maybe we missed the signal. I knew we didn't "have to have" the lot.

I said, "Look, we made a deal this morning and shook hands. If it is God's sovereign will for us to have this lot, then there is nothing you or I can do to prevent it from happening. However, if it is not God's will for us to have this lot, then no amount of me begging and pleading with you or with him right now is going to make it happen. So you go ahead and do what you need to do."

There was a long pause on the other end of the line. "Well, okay," he said. "Since you put it like that, you've got the lot."

To be a good steward is to give God that last word on everything you do. He has a plan for your life. The Bible says, "To man belong the plans of the heart, but from the LORD comes the reply of the tongue" (Proverbs 16:1). God's will and plan will prevail. So you can trust him fully. On the other hand, God typically doesn't show us his plan in advance; most often he reveals it step by step. Not knowing exactly how the script will turn out, we must be responsible to do our part.

To be a good steward, a noble manager, of what God has given to us means to trust in his sovereign plan and to faithfully take every step he reveals to us along the way. Happiness is the by-product of submitting to this process of stewardship.

Stewardship Isn't Easy

Living at the "end" of a dirt road has its advantages. It's like living in the middle of the country, even though we're five minutes from downtown. Our neighbors, however, live "on" a dirt road, and for them the dust was wreaking havoc. Also, the high cost of regularly grading the road posed a problem for the county road department.

Therefore, I wasn't surprised to learn that several neighbors had drummed up support for the county to pave our road. Frankly, I liked the dirt road just fine, but I sure understood where both neighbors and the county administrators were coming from.

One day I learned, however, that the county was planning to use a less expensive paving treatment of gravel mixed with tar that goes down soft, then hardens. When I found out that this treatment could be accomplished at one-fifth the cost of a "regular" paving job, I was naturally concerned about the effect on property values. Also, because we're paying one hundred percent of the property taxes I couldn't see why we should have to accept twenty percent of a real road. In fact, the project was to be carried out by the county's road "maintenance" department. So they were going to have men who run road graders and who patch potholes actually engineer and build the road.

Terrified, I asked for some samples of similar roads. After visiting them I had apoplexy. I could visualize our neighborhood looking like a tenement. Except for one kindred spirit, all my neighbors were so thrilled to have the road paved at all that they were willing to overlook what I considered several serious flaws in the plan.

Now this one neighbor who shared my concerns was a spiritually curious man with whom I had been talking about Jesus. I called him up, told him what I was thinking, and said, "We need to think through what would be the right thing to do here." After tossing out a number of reasonable ideas, I added, "I guess we also need to consider whatever legal recourse we might have."

My neighbor shot back, "Oh! So then, you're a Christian with a big stick?!"

I must admit that rocked me a bit, and I gave him a weak reply, so weak in fact that I conveniently cannot remember to this day what it was.

For the next twenty-four hours I stewed over his comment. I realized there were two issues creating spiritual tension here. On one hand, my neighbors, except for this one gentleman, wanted the road paved. They didn't mind what it would look like as long as it made the dust go away. And I was genuinely sympathetic to the problem of dust.

Because I am a Christian, I experienced what we might call "neighbor love." "Love God...love your neighbor." Neighbor love was clearly one of the spiritual dynamics at work in this conundrum.

On the other hand, there is also the spiritual dynamic of stewardship. I have been entrusted with certain things—including watching out for our property value. But these relationships with neighbors are also part of what I've been entrusted with.

The next day I called my neighbor back and said, "I think I've got this sorted out. We have tension here between being faithful stewards of that with which we've been entrusted and being good neighbors who show neighbor love, which is the other spiritual dynamic at work here." Thankfully, he seemed satisfied with my analysis.

As it turned out, I expressed so much concern to the county road department about the quality of the road that an additional crew of several men came to watch over the actual paving job. In the end it turned out fine, considering the cost.

SECRET #6
STEWARDSHIP

For most of us, the idea of *stewardship* is like a mothballed sweater only pulled out of our vocabulary closet during the annual "stewardship campaign" at church (read: "give more money"). We cringe at its mere mention because we expect a verbal spanking about tithing or the lack thereof. Biblical stewardship encompasses money, but so much more. Biblically, everything we have comes from God.

Stewardship is a total way of looking at life which understands that everything comes from God, belongs to God, and is to be used for the glory of God. A steward will come to believe that God has a "plan" for his life — that God has ordained all his days before one of them came to pass, that God determines his times and even the exact places where he lives (see Psalm 139:16; Acts 17:26). A steward knows that he has enough time to complete every task God intends him to do. A steward does not have to worry about the future because he knows that God is not only good but also sovereignly in control. A steward knows that God will not fail to complete the good work — the "plan" — he has begun (see Philippians 1:6).

Unfortunately, this rich historical idea of stewardship has largely fallen into disuse, which makes the already difficult job of being a good steward all the more difficult. Stewardship is not a series of clear "up or down" decisions we make. Stewardship is complicated. Stewardship involves every decision we make, because every decision allocates the "limited" time, abilities, and money we have to "spend."

So, if you want to be truly happy, you must become a "biblical" steward. Remember: If you will do what you don't want to do, you will become what you want to be. Now let's turn our attention to how these ideas work themselves out in everyday living.

Money and Possessions

Beyond exhorting us to share with the church and with the poor and urging us not to make money a god, the Bible gives us great freedom with respect to our money and possessions. While all things are permissible, however, not all things will leave us happy. Here are several ideas—not all of them will apply to everyone, but you may find them to be worth considering where they are relevant to your life. You can add to the list, I'm sure.

First, don't own things you do not use on a regular basis. Recently I heard of a man who owns three homes—a city home, an island estate, and a Florida condominium. He commented that for twenty years his family celebrated the Fourth of July weekend by opening up their island home. His children are grown and married now, but they and their families still converge for that special weekend.

For years he and his wife went to the property a few days ahead of time to kill mice, hack back vegetation, stock the shelves, rig the utilities, and so on. Last year, however, he just couldn't face up to the tasks, so he asked one of his sons and his family to go in early and take care of preparing the property. It's no longer fun for him.

If a man owns three homes—or four—and he uses all of them, and God has blessed him so it's not financially imprudent, it's a wonderful thing.

For me personally, however, I made a decision twenty-five years ago not to own anything I don't use on a regular basis.

For seven years we owned a weekend lake house just outside of town. Virtually every Friday afternoon we would "kidnap" our children and spend the weekend doing country things.

When our daughter turned eleven, though, her in-town friends became very important to her. We only went to the lake house once that year, so we decided to sell the property to a neighbor who had expressed an interest in purchasing it. There was nothing wrong with owning the property; there was no requirement to sell the property; there was no special virtue to own or not own the property. The process of evaluating our use of this house did, however, keep us lean and responsive to God's leading in our lives.

During and after the time we owned the weekend lake house, we lived in a suburban home with a tennis court and swimming pool. We used them all the time, but then for a few years for a variety of reasons we just didn't take the time to play tennis or go swimming. So we sold the home to a family who now enjoys them very much. And because we missed being around the water, we moved our primary residence to a home on a lake.

There is no particular virtue in not enjoying what blessings God allows. There is no particular virtue in living below your means. But there is virtue in carefully evaluating how we manage what is entrusted to our care.

This idea—to not own anything you don't use on a regular basis—is not for everyone. Nor does it make one man more spiritual than another. However, it has freed me up tremendously. Why? Everything you and I own requires spending a certain amount of time, money, and anxiety on maintenance—not to mention a certain opportunity cost. Every hour we spend mowing or cleaning means an hour we won't spend reading a good book or tossing a ball with our kids. Sometimes we have to make difficult choices. Sometimes the best thing we can do is this: Do what we don't want to do so we can become what we want to be.

Second, don't own things just because you can. A neighbor about a mile down the shore from us owns a wood 1957 Chris-Craft Sportsman inboard boat. Simply put, it's magnificent! He has completely restored the mahogany to its original luster. I love the throaty purr of the antique Chris-Craft engine when he drives by.

Three years ago I had mentioned to him that I would be interested if he ever wanted to sell his boat. Then, six months ago, I noticed he wasn't taking the boat out anymore. After a number of weeks had passed I stopped by one day, found out he was having some family health problems, and once again mentioned my interest.

Over a two-week period we agreed on what I considered a fair price, subject to a test drive and my ability to become comfortable with the boat. We took the boat out for a spin. As it turned out, lack of use had left the boat needing several repairs. He agreed to have the problems fixed, and then we would take another test drive. Because the mechanic was busy, it took nearly a month to have the repairs made.

During that time I continued to pray about selling our boat to buy the antique Chris-Craft. One day the question came to mind, "Why not deny yourself this boat?" Because I had been thinking about this boat for three years, that thought came as quite a jolt. However, I had also been wondering if I should buy it just because I had enough money to do so.

Over a period of several days I came to the conclusion that, for me, it would be a good lesson in self-restraint and personal discipline to forgo the purchase. The seller was disappointed, but I felt a tremendous release in my spirit. On the other hand, there were other purchases I was considering at the time with which I went ahead and felt just fine doing so. Do what you don't want to do and you will become what you want to be.

Third, the more you give away the happier you will be. Because Man in the Mirror is a 501(C)3 charitable organization, we receive financial gifts from donors. Over the years I have developed beautiful friendships with many of these donors. Here is an iron law about donors: The greater proportion of their income they give, the happier they are. I believe this is well attested by Scripture.

On the other hand, I'm reminded of the day I asked a man with a net worth of approximately $5,000,000 if he would help fund a particular project. He said, "Patrick, I would love to help you. But I just don't feel like I can right now. I'm trying to get myself to a point where I'll feel financially secure." After further discussion, it became clear he was only giving the minimum possible amount to charitable and religious causes—and then largely because of social and business pressures.

Ironically, for some men it's almost as if the more money they have, the more afraid they are that it's going to run out. If that has been your concern, I believe the Bible makes it clear that if you are generous toward others, God will be generous toward you. You are not going to run out of money.

Many men have concluded that the concept of tithing—giving away ten percent of your income—is an Old Testament idea that no longer applies. It certainly is an Old Testament idea, as these two passages illustrate:

> *Honor the LORD with your wealth, with the firstfruits of all your crops; then your barns will be filled to overflowing, and your vats will brim over with new wine.*
>
> PROVERBS 3:9–10

> *"Bring the whole tithe into the storehouse, that there may be food in my house. Test me in this," says the LORD Almighty, "and see if I will not throw open the floodgates of heaven and pour out so much blessing that you will not have room enough for it."*
>
> MALACHI 3:10

Yet, tithing is also a New Testament concept, fully ratified by Jesus himself. Jesus was never more angry than when he dressed down the religious leaders of his day in Matthew 23. Look at one thing he said:

Woe to you, teachers of the law and Pharisees, you hypocrites!
You give a tenth of your spices—mint, dill and cummin. But you have
neglected the more important matters of the law—justice, mercy and
faithfulness. You should have practiced the latter, without neglecting
the former.

MATTHEW 23:23

Jesus said, in essence, "Look at you! You scrupulously give ten percent of every little nickel you earn, but you're careless about your
behavior! You need to add ethical behavior, *without neglecting the*
tithing you already do." A wise man will see what he must see. Also, a
shrewd man will not fail to see the promises in the two Old Testament
passages above.

Family

Carl spends more hours than seems reasonable pulling his two
sons behind a ski boat. They ski everywhere. They ski all the time. For
fun. For competition. One day I had the opportunity and mustered up
the courage to ask him why he spends so much time with his boys.

He answered, "Well, I watched my neighbor raise his two boys. He
never spent much time with them. Those boys got involved in drugs
and alcohol. And now in his later years, he spends most of his time and
money trying to rehabilitate his boys. So I realized I could either choose
a large gas bill for my boat now, or a large rehab bill later, and I decided
to spend the money on fuel now."

The idea is to steward our time for the priorities we do have, not
the ones we wish we had. When you father a child, or say "I do" to the
solemn vow of marriage, that creates responsibility. A steward is
responsible to be faithful to that for which he is accountable. We are

not accountable for the set of responsibilities we wish we had, but for the set of responsibilities we do have.

Rest and Health

A pastor is much like a businessman. He must offer vision, provide direction, give leadership, identify talented people, mobilize workers, and much, much more. And like every businessman, every pastor longs for a dynamic, successful work.

People expect their pastor to give scintillating sermons, run an administratively efficient office, work effectively with a staff, meet an ambitious budget, maintain a physical plant, attend every committee meeting (which of course always take place during nonbusiness hours), perform all weddings and funerals, counsel parishioners in their troubles and visit them in their illnesses, be a dynamic and visionary leader, have no ego, and maintain a perfectly balanced marriage and family life.

Is it any wonder that many pastors are discouraged? They are not necessarily tired "of" ministry, but they are certainly tired "in" ministry. Why? Well, often it's because a church, like a business or challenging profession, is an insatiable mistress. Many men, pastors or not, are tired "in" what they do, and at least in some cases, they are tired "of" what they do.

Unless we balance the demands of our own private and public lives we will eventually hit the wall. No one else can, or should, take on this responsibility for us. And if we do hit the wall, the people who drove us there will feel sorry for us, but they won't feel responsible. On the contrary, in the same way a congregation expects their pastor to take responsibility for his life, both publicly and privately, our customers, associates, and friends expect us to take responsibility for ours. This is at the heart of what it means to be a faithful steward, and being a faithful steward is at the heart of being a happy man. If you will do what you don't want to do, you will become what you want to be.

Focus Questions

1. How much stress are you under from your circumstances? To what extent do you feel an excessive stress level may be the result of not taking responsibility for your own life?

2. What does it mean that God is sovereign? Why is the sovereignty of God such an enormous comfort when it looks like life may go in a different direction than we want it to go?

3. "If it is God's sovereign will for something to happen, then there is nothing you or anyone else can do to prevent it from happening. However, if it is not God's will, then no amount of begging and pleading is going to make it happen." Do you agree? Why? How can this principle make you a more confident steward?

4. Is there something you don't use on a regular basis that you might be better off selling? Is there something you own just because you can, even though you really don't need it? Do you give ten percent of your income to God's work?

5. Have you thought about your family as a stewardship? What would be a benefit to thinking this way?

6. Are you getting enough rest? Are you managing your schedule and the demands that other people put on you?

7. What is the major decision you're facing right now? What have you learned as you read this chapter that can give you greater confidence in making that decision?

CHAPTER SEVEN

WE FIND OUR HAPPINESS
BY HELPING OTHERS
FIND THEIRS

7

WE FIND OUR HAPPINESS BY
HELPING OTHERS FIND THEIRS

As we search for happiness we observe that most men are not. Ironically, one way God completes our own happiness is by helping other men find theirs. True happiness, meaning, and purpose is only found in God, so to help a man find happiness is to help him find God.

In this chapter we'll take a careful look at the different ways men are learning to tell others the good story about Jesus Christ.

Some time ago a friend of mine was hired to consult with Dream-Works on their blockbuster movie *The Prince of Egypt.* His task was to comment on whether the movie was staying true to the Christian sensibility.

During the course of getting acquainted, the DreamWorks staff wanted to know exactly what makes a Christian. After my friend explained what it means to be a Christian, and how to become one, a puzzled employee asked, "You mean *anyone* can become a Christian?"

The good news about Jesus Christ is the most hopeful story a man can ever hear. Yet even in our religiously saturated society, many only know Jesus through gross caricatures, brief sound bites, unfair stereotypes, and faulty spokesmen. The worth of an idea shouldn't be judged by its worst examples, but people do tend to judge Christianity by its most silly adherents. That's why you, as a "normal" person, are such a valuable spokesman—you have the ability to catch men off guard as you present the truth of the gospel.

Changing Your Story

When football superstar Dion Sanders played for the Atlanta Falcons he gained a reputation as a premier punt returner. On one occasion after returning a punt for a touchdown, Sanders purchased Gucci watches for the entire punt return team as a way to show his appreciation for the crucial role they played in his success.

Some time later Sanders became a follower of Jesus Christ. The story is told of the day when Sanders, as a member of the Dallas Cowboys, had again returned a punt for a touchdown. A Cowboys teammate, who had coincidentally played with Dion in Atlanta, remembered the watch incident and asked him, "Hey Dion, are you going to do it again?"

"No," said Dion, "I'm going to buy everybody an NIV Bible."

Now why would Dion Sanders give an answer like that? God changed his story. A man who experiences a great restaurant can't wait to tell his friends about it; he wants them to give it a try. In a much greater way, a man who experiences Jesus Christ can't wait to tell his friends about it; he wants his friends to give God a try. The greatest gift a man can ever receive is to know Jesus Christ as Savior and Lord.

Deciding Which Story to Tell

In the early years of my business career my hero was Trammel Crow, arguably the greatest real estate developer of our time.

As a young real estate developer just getting started, I desperately wanted to meet this great man. For several years I had tried to schedule an appointment with Mr. Crow. I was rebuffed at every attempt, never able to get beyond his secretary. Finally, after receiving my calls quarterly for several years, his secretary said to me one day, "Mr. Morley, when are you going to get it through your head? Mr. Crow is very busy with his own projects. He's just simply not going to be able to meet with you." Well, I may be slow, but I got the message. I never called again. But he was still my hero.

In the meantime, my own business grew. I was blessed to be able to become a member of the Urban Land Institute, the most prestigious trade association for developers. Then the unbelievable happened. The Urban Land Institute scheduled its major convention in my hometown of Orlando, Florida. Mr. Crow was scheduled to speak as part of a roundtable discussion.

I fantasized about renting a billboard between the airport and the convention headquarters hotel, which would read, "Morley Properties welcomes Trammel Crow and the Urban Land Institute to Orlando!"

On a more practical note, I registered for the roundtable in which Mr. Crow would participate. I planned to arrive thirty minutes early so I could sit in the front row. Then after the session I would be the first one to rush forward to speak to him.

Next I started to think about what I would say to this great man. For weeks, as I drove around town during the day, I turned it over in my mind. I thought to myself, *Within a few moments after adjournment he will be swamped with well-wishers. You only have one brief shot. Better to ask him a question. Since you only have time for one question, what will it be? What is the one, big, magical question that can unlock the secret of his success?*

Over and over, round and round I went. The big day fast approaching, I racked my brain, but I just couldn't think of anything very significant, especially given the little time I would have.

About a week before the conference it hit me. There was nothing Trammel Crow could tell me in the course of a minute that would help me one little bit; there just wasn't enough time. It occurred to me then to stop thinking about what I could get from him. In a flash of inspiration, I decided what I would say.

Because I arrived so early on the big day, I was able to sit in the front row, directly in front of Mr. Crow's nameplate. The room slowly filled and the meeting began and ran smoothly toward its conclusion. At the instant the chairman's gavel adjourned the meeting, I shot up to where Mr. Crow was seated.

"Mr. Crow, my name is Pat Morley," I began. "I know I only have time for one quick question, so here it is. I'm a follower of Jesus Christ and I was wondering if anyone has ever talked to you about what it means to be born again."

With his trademark twinkle, he bent over, grabbed the name tag pinned to my chest and said, "Let me see now. What's your name? Pat. Yes, I think I know what you're getting at. I do believe in God but probably not in the same way you do."

"Well, Mr. Crow. I know that you are familiar with Dr. Bill Bright. He's written a small booklet entitled *The Four Spiritual Laws*, which explains how a man can have his sins forgiven and receive God's gift of eternal life. I would like to give you a copy." Reaching forward I continued, "Here is the booklet with my business card, just in case you would ever want to talk further about this."

In characteristically charming fashion, Mr. Crow thanked me profusely, stuffed the booklet and card into his shirt pocket, then was overtaken by the mob. Not that I was expecting it, but I never heard from or saw him again after that day.

Storytelling Jitters

Nothing could be more desirable, or perhaps more nerve-racking, than to tell the good story of our own faith in Jesus Christ. And it is a good story. Yet there are a lot of obstacles that can stand in the way. Consider these reasons why some of us hesitate to tell others about what the Lord has done for us. You may be able to add more of your own:

◆ "I know I should be witnessing more. I have the desire, but I don't do it. I allow other things to get in the way."

◆ "I just don't feel like it's my responsibility."

◆ "I don't know any non-Christians."

◆ "I'm too busy. I just can't afford to take the time."

◆ "It's just easier to not risk offending someone."

◆ "It feels so uncomfortable. I would be so embarrassed."

◆ "I've had a bad experience, and I just don't want to take the risk again."

◆ "It could be too costly to my career."

◆ "I've been told not to talk about religion at work."

◆ "I feel ill-equipped to witness. I just don't know what to say."

◆ "Me? You're kidding! Who would ever want to listen to me?"

◆ "The thought is too terrifying to me. I could never do it."

In the meantime, men are asking or, more usually, thinking about these profound questions:

◆ How can I resolve the bitterness and anger inside me?

◆ What do I do with the loneliness and emptiness I feel?

- ◆ How can I handle the guilt I feel?

- ◆ What would it take for me to be a happy person?

- ◆ Is there any meaning to life? What is it?

- ◆ What is the purpose of my life?

- ◆ In a world of relativism, what is true?

- ◆ Why is life so hard?

- ◆ What will happen when I die?

Ironically, within a hundred yards of where you sit are many, many men who need to hear the good news about Jesus—if only someone would incarnate the story, then proclaim it to them.

Showing the Good Story

Longshoreman philosopher Lech Walesa is reported to have once said, "There is a declining world market for words." Framed in slightly different words, people are tired of hearing. They want to see.

We have longtime friends who live in Atlanta, Georgia. On a Maundy Thursday some time ago, the day before Good Friday, a violent tornado ripped down their street, destroying just about everything in its path.

Our friends had a hundred trees in their backyard. Every single one of them was blown down. During the tornado's onslaught, our friends sat in their home, which, ironically and mercifully, remained mostly untouched and undamaged. Yet next door and up and down the street, homes of neighbors were severely battered.

One home on the street was totally destroyed. Fortunately, that family was away on vacation. Had they been home they would have been killed.

A man who is a Christian lives on their street. He decided to mobilize area churches to provide help to the community. He went door to door, ruin to ruin, canvassing the neighborhood to take inventory of their needs.

Then he contacted the many churches that had expressed interest, and people began streaming into the neighborhood to bring relief. They brought meals, hauled away trash, and provided child care for the children. Everyone in the devastated community was overwhelmed with gratitude. They saw just how good the good story can be.

The apostle Paul once wrote, "We loved you so much that we were delighted to share with you not only the gospel of God but our lives as well" (1 Thessalonians 2:8). He understood the importance of "telling" the good story — "we were delighted to share . . . the gospel." This is *proclamation*. He also understood the importance of "showing" the good story — "we were delighted to share . . . our lives as well." This is *incarnation*.

Proclamation and *incarnation*. In a word-saturated world people are saying more and more, "First show me. Then, when I have come to trust you, you can tell me." A man's receptivity to what we "proclaim" will rarely exceed the authenticity of how we actually live.

Our Convictions About Telling the Good Story

Over the years I have come to an odd conclusion: Men do exactly what they want to do. And this includes men who work for you. Basically, we all do what we believe to be true. Because our beliefs help determine our behavior, what should we believe to be true about our responsibility for telling the good story? There are many possibilities, but consider these few (and you may think of others to add):

◆ *The single most important need people have is to know Jesus Christ personally.* "Salvation is found in no one else, for there is no other name under heaven given to men by which we must be saved" (Acts 4:12).

◆ *A Christian should feel a certain sense of urgency to tell the good story.* When reminded, "Didn't we tell you not to speak or teach in this name?" Peter and John replied, "Judge for yourselves whether it is right in God's sight to obey you rather than God. For we cannot help speaking about what we have seen and heard" (Acts 4:19–20).

◆ *People will only listen to someone they trust.* That being the case, "Be wise in the way you act toward outsiders; make the most of every opportunity. Let your conversation be always full of grace, seasoned with salt, so that you may know how to answer everyone" (Colossians 4:5–6).

◆ *People will consider us credible on the basis of their values, not ours. Therefore, we must earn their respect by the way we live.* "Make it your ambition to lead a quiet life, to mind your own business and to work with your hands, just as we told you, so that your daily life may win the respect of outsiders and so that you will not be dependent on anybody" (1 Thessalonians 4:11–12).

◆ *To speak well we must prepare in advance.* "Always be prepared to give an answer to everyone who asks you to give the reason for the hope that you have. But do this with gentleness and respect" (1 Peter 3:15).

If these statements are true, do you personally believe them? If you believe them, is there a one-to-one correlation between your belief and your behavior? If not, you may want to consider spending some time trying to align your Bible, your belief, and your behavior.

Telling the Good Story at Walmart

There are two broad groups of shoppers at Walmart. First are those who know Jesus Christ and have a fundamental peace and joy in their hearts. Second are those filled with worries, frustrations, and doubts—some who know Christ, but most who do not.

Imagine you're walking down an aisle at Walmart. As you survey the people you pass on the way, you notice that some seem joyful, but most don't seem very happy, or at the very least they seem preoccupied.

Suppose the store manager's voice boomed out over the loudspeaker: "Okay, shoppers! Today in place of our blue-light special we're going to do something a little different. First, we have some shoppers today who are filled with peace and joy because they have a personal relationship with Jesus Christ. Now, I want everyone who knows Jesus to raise your hand!" About one-third of the hands go up.

"Good, that's good! Okay, you can put your hands down. Now we also have some shoppers with us today who are a little down, a little depressed. They don't know God—or they do but now they've lost the joy of their salvation. If you're here today and your life isn't turning out like you hoped, I want you to raise your hand. Okay, good, good!

"Now leave them up for just a minute. Now, I want all you shoppers who know Jesus Christ and have a joyful life to find someone with their hand up and tell them the good story about your life and how they too can know Jesus personally for the first time, or if they've known him but have walked away from him—how their relationship with him can be restored."

We could fulfill the Great Commission (Matthew 28:19–20) in twenty-four hours!

Through every crowd drift men and women hungry and thirsty for God. In every crowd God has stationed men and women who hold the bread of life and the cup of living water. What would happen if we could get them talking together?

Too often, way too often, however, they swirl suspiciously around each other, sizing each other up, never touching, never talking about that which is real, then go away feeling incomplete and diminished for the experience.

The non-Christian feels incomplete because a spiritual cancer eats away at his soul. The Christian feels incomplete because he has demonstrated that his faith is inauthentic. God feels incomplete because his word—which according to his promise in Isaiah 55:11 accomplishes what he desires and achieves the purpose for which he sends it—falls silent for a time in a dark place.

Two Minutes Late Is Too Late

It was the day of the annual Thanksgiving Leadership Prayer Breakfast in Orlando. After the breakfast program had concluded, I drove our very distinguished guest speaker to the airport so he could catch his flight back home.

He suggested that we grab some lunch before heading to the gate, so we went to a comfortable restaurant inside the airport. As we sat down, I asked the waiter if he could have us out in twenty-five minutes, which he assured me he could do. At the appropriate time we walked out the door. We passed through security, boarded a tram to the airline terminal, then walked at a comfortable pace to the gate.

When my guest presented his ticket for a boarding pass the gate agent said, "I'm sorry, sir, but we have a full flight with several standbys. Since you weren't here at the ten-minute cutoff point, we gave your seat away two minutes ago."

"What!" we said simultaneously as we both physically fell back in shock. "That can't be. Here's the ticket. There must be some way to resolve this," appealed the out-of-town visitor.

The gate agent, while not surly, offered little sympathy and no help. After several more jousts I said, "Look, you don't understand. This is the most important person in Orlando today. He has to be on that flight. I will buy a ticket in first class!"

"First class is sold out," she said, immovably trenchant.

At this point, embarrassed to the marrow, I said impulsively, "Then I'll give $1,000 to a volunteer to give up their seat. This man has to be on this flight!"

After several minutes of sparring, we watched helplessly as another agent closed the door that led down the Jetway to the plane's interior. At that point she suggested we talk to her supervisor. By now you realize what happened. He missed the plane, and it was one hundred percent entirely and completely my fault. It ranks as one of the ten most humiliating moments of my life.

This story illustrates a worthwhile point. If you are strolling through life, thinking you have plenty of time, but get to the door after the deadline of decision to surrender your life to Jesus, it doesn't make any difference how important you are. Once the door to eternal life is shut, you're not going to get in. Two minutes late is too late. There is an end to grace.

SECRET #7
WITNESSING

Probably within a hundred yards of where you are now reading these words are a dozen men eaten up by the futility of their lives. The single most important need people have is to know Jesus Christ as their Savior and Lord. At the same time, few things in life are more nerve-racking than sharing our faith in Jesus Christ. Ironically, many men are dying to know what we are dying not to tell them. A true believer, however, will overcome these fears and feel a sense of urgency and responsibility to help men find faith — because there is an end to grace. The happiest men in the world are witnessing Christians. They experience the nearly indescribable joy of watching broken men become healed.

What Holds Us Back

I've often wondered how men can be spiritually apathetic about their neighbors and coworkers. Recently a thought struck me that must surely provide at least part of the answer:

We don't care about people we don't know.

When you get to know someone personally, you first begin to observe the thin veneer of "things are great." Later, though, if the relationship deepens beyond superficial conversations about "news, sports, and the weather," the rest of the picture slowly begins to fill in.

You learn of the aches and pains, the disappointments and heartaches, the sufferings and sorrows, the futility and frustrations, the fears and anxieties, the loneliness and emptiness, the dread of a looming crisis. You feel the pain of broken marriages, the sadness of a child breaking a heart, the anguish of a business failing, the bitterness of a loyal and hardworking employee being passed over for a promotion.

We must engage and not withdraw from the "real" lives of the people we know. If we learn anything from observing the life of Jesus it is this: Our message is not merely proclamation, but also incarnation. When Paul said, "We loved you so much that we were delighted to share with you not only the gospel of God but our lives as well . . ." he also told us why: " . . . *because you had become so dear to us"* (1 Thessalonians 2:8, italics added).

Our spiritual interest in others will be in direct proportion to how well we get to know them personally.

So I'm not suggesting you need to be a better witness (to do so, you see, will only make you feel even more guilty). Rather, why not begin building some deep, meaningful personal relationships with lost men. Then after you get to "really" know them, love will compel you to share the difference Jesus has made in your life—and can make in theirs.

You'll never be more interested in someone's salvation than when you're interested in them personally.

Because there is an end to grace, there should also be an end to apathy.

What Holds Us Back #2

We will also not share the good story if we have not been long enough and deep enough in the presence of Jesus. For some of us, we must confess this painful truth: He has not overwhelmed us—we have not let him do so. We look like a smoldering fire died down. When once we have been in the real presence of Jesus, tongues of fire will leap from us, dance about, then lick out at those who dare to stand too close—those who hope that they too might have their hearts set on fire for the Lord.

That which is true, real, authentic will break out in light and salty speech. We cannot help but speak of him. When once we have been "with Jesus," he will be our first and best thought in every situation. Our words become the healing words of Jesus himself. Those who hurt become like a little bird with a broken wing, healed and set free.

An Updated Approach to Witnessing

The simple fact that all men desire to believe in something means something. Consider the following claims; ponder how you might apply them to those who may be receptive to the good story you have to tell:

◆ **Relationship: We must fully understand what the non-believer is saying so he can say of us, "Yes, that's what I'm saying — you understand my position." Only then will he be willing to hear what we have to say.**

◆ Relevance: We must address the questions nonbelievers are asking, not the questions they are not asking. People are trying to solve their problems, not ours. What does that mean for us? Simply this: We must keep up with the ideas and issues floating around in our culture.

◆ Truth: We must be relevant while never compromising what is real and what is true. Give men what they need in the context of what they want. Francis Schaeffer wrote, "Each generation of the church in each setting has the responsibility of communicating the gospel in understandable terms, considering the language and thought-forms of that setting."[1]

◆ Credibility: We must apply a rigorous scholarship that keeps up with the current thinking and the most recent research. A lot of men don't know what they're talking about, but that doesn't seem to stop them from talking about it anyway. Be cautious when the argument for something is no stronger than the argument against it.

◆ Conversation: A generation ago men would sit and listen to a speaker offer a *propositional* Jesus. No longer is that true. Today men want to have a conversation — a dialogue — about a *relational* Jesus.

---

1. Francis A. Schaeffer, *Escape from Reason* (Downer's Grove, Ill.: InterVarsity Press, 1968), 94.

Here's how to get 6 months free MSN Internet Access:

Call 1-800-FREE-MSN, ext. 118, to sign up for one year of MSN Internet Access and get 6 months free.

Or complete and return this card to receive your MSN set-up software CD.

Phone Number (_____) _____ E-mail _____

☐ Would you like to receive a call from an MSN Representative to sign you up?

Name _____

Address _____

City/State _____ ZIP _____

Do you currently receive Internet access from a provider other than MSN?
☐ No ☐ Yes If yes, who is your current provider?
☐ America Online ☐ EarthLink/Sprint ☐ AT&T WorldNet
☐ MCI WorldCom ☐ Other _____

How many monthly hours do you receive through your current subscription?
☐ 0–30 ☐ 30–100 ☐ 100–300 ☐ Unlimited ☐ Other _____

msn
The Everyday Web.™

· Fewer disconnects*

· Free 24/7 customer support

· Smart, relevant search results

· E-mail that goes where you go

· Instantly talk to your online friends

· Share photos and information

First 6 Months
Internet Access FREE
1-800-FREE MSN

Men Would Witness More If . . .

Most men have it in their hearts to do the right things. Witnessing is one of those things. Assuming we have broken through the barrier of lack of desire, we will witness more if we:

Have something to give men. If you have read a book that was meaningful to you, and it does a good job of explaining and promoting the Christian faith, why not adopt a ministry of giving that book to men in need. You might even consider selecting several different books for different types of needs and crises.

Have somewhere to send men. In most cities there are men who regularly lead other men to Jesus Christ. They probably teach Bible studies or lead small groups. They may periodically organize prayer breakfasts. They may take men to lunch to share their faith stories. They may be laymen or pastors. Learn who these men are. Establish contact. Get to know them personally. Then, when you have a man who needs spiritual help, you will have a place to send or bring them.

Have something to say to men. Most men are terrified to talk about their faith. Why? Most likely because they lack confidence and experience. The best way to gain confidence and experience is to receive hands-on training about how to share your faith. Your church may offer such a course. If not, find out who in your community offers such training, or contact Evangelism Explosion International at 954−491−6100.

Have a plan to reach men. In the same way your business would flounder if you didn't have a goal and a strategy to reach the goal, you will most likely not effectively witness without a goal and a strategy. You may want to consider the idea known simply as *Reach 3.* The idea is as simple as it sounds. Prayerfully write down the names of three friends, coworkers, or neighbors. Pray for their salvation. Invite each to a no-agenda lunch. Build a relationship. Take them to outreach events. We at Man in the Mirror produce wallet-sized "Reach 3" cards, which you can order in quantities at no charge by contacting our office at 407–331–0095.

We don't have to "fix" men. We have some friends who held a party some time ago at which everyone dressed up as witches, goblins, and the like. We chose not to tell them that their choice of party theme was bad; we simply chose not to go. In telling the good story of Jesus it's important that we not tell men how to live their lives. If we instead focus on teaching them the principles, the Holy Spirit will make the applications come alive in them.

The happiest men I've known have been witnessing Christians. They understand that Christianity is Jesus Christ, who is the way and the truth and the life. Everyone is invited to step inside the circle—Hindus and Buddhists, agnostics and atheists, Republicans and Democrats, Jews and Gentiles, men and women, rich and poor, red and yellow, straight and gay, evangelicals and fundamentalists, mainliners and Pentecostals, Presbyterians and Baptists, Catholics and Episcopalians.

FOCUS QUESTIONS

1. **How confident or nervous are you about sharing your faith story with other men? Why is that? Which of the bullet points under the heading "Storytelling Jitters" apply to you?**

2. **What are your beliefs about what happens to people who don't know Jesus Christ as their Savior? What are your beliefs about how people are saved? What are your beliefs about how people are introduced to salvation? Do your behaviors reflect your beliefs?**

3. **If in question #2 you answered that your behavior doesn't match your belief, what could, should, and would you do to change that?**

4. Review the ideas in the section titled "An Updated Approach to Witnessing." Which of these ideas is new to you? Explain how embracing this idea can change your behavior.

5. Men will witness more if they have something to give, somewhere to send, and something to say. What steps could you take to accomplish each of these three actions?

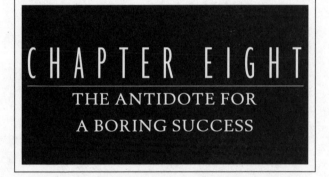

CHAPTER EIGHT

THE ANTIDOTE FOR
A BORING SUCCESS

◆

8

THE ANTIDOTE FOR A BORING SUCCESS

A bumper sticker seen recently: Jesus is coming. Look busy.

We hosted a dinner party at our home a while ago at which a number of people met each other for the first time. After dinner I offered a word of introduction about each guest.

Among our guests were Dr. Charles McKenzie, my philosophy professor, and his wife. When I came to this man, I stumbled. "When I think of Dr. McKenzie . . ." I said. "How would I put this?"

Then I heard these words come out of my mouth: "It's like this. Everyone is trying to get where they want to go. Every now and then you meet someone who wants to help you get where you want to go. When you're around that person for a while, you think to yourself, 'I want to be like that.' Dr. McKenzie is that kind of person."

This chapter explores what it means to be "that kind of person."

The Agony of Self

Kyle said, "I'm twenty-eight years old. My wife and I love each other deeply. We both work, we like our work, we're making good money, and we have every material thing we want. My relationship with the Lord is good—I've been a Christian for seven years.

"But I told my wife last week: 'You know, we get up, make the bed, go to work, come home, make dinner, wash dishes, clean the house, relax a little, go to bed, then get up the next morning and do it all over again. It's all so boring.'" Looking straight at me he said, "What's the point?"

After posing a few exploratory questions I asked Kyle what he was doing to serve the Lord. He said, "You know, I'm really not doing anything to serve God. Actually, come to think of it, everything in my life has been focused on me—getting what I want, meeting my needs, advancing my career."

After a few more minutes, Kyle began to see that he was "getting" from God but "giving" nothing in return. He made this interesting observation: "Recently I've been telling my wife I think I'm supposed to become a leader. Now I know what that's about." We discussed ways he could discover his spiritual gifts, then network with his pastor and with his contacts in the workplace to find an opportunity to "serve God by serving others."

You could look at serving others this way: Because the lane is narrow on this road of surrender, obedience, and service, a fellow traveler broken and beaten down by the blows of life is hard to walk around. Indeed, one feels compelled by the love of Jesus Christ to lend a hand. Serving God by serving others keeps traffic from backing up along the way.

It is by taking the narrow road of giving that we end up on the broad road of receiving. Jesus put it this way: "If you obey my commands, you will remain in my love, just as I have obeyed my Father's commands and remain in his love. I have told you this so that my joy may be in you and that your joy may be complete" (John 15:10–11).

SECRET #8
SERVICE

Stage one of Christian growth is to become a *learner* — a disciple. Once we begin to understand the breadth of God's love and grace, though, and feel a deepening gratitude, stage two of continuing Christian growth is to become a *worker* — a servant. What is a servant? *A servant is someone who goes where Jesus would go to do what Jesus would do.* Where would Jesus go? What would Jesus do? Unless and until we serve him as an expression of gratitude, our lives will have no enduring meaning. We will not be happy.

Green Grapes

Many years ago I was listening to an audiotape of a sermon, and I heard an illustration that has flashed into my mind on perhaps a hundred different occasions. (I apologize that I do not recall the name of the pastor—let me know if you know him.)

This pastor told of the time he was walking down a sidewalk, eating some green grapes. As he passed by a homeless man begging for loose change, the thought passed through the pastor's mind, "Why don't you give that man your grapes?"

Now the pastor was hungry himself. He had really been looking forward to snacking on those grapes. He really didn't want to give them up. They tasted good in his mouth—very refreshing. He thought to himself, "Lord, I really want to eat these grapes, but if I'm supposed to give these grapes to this man then that's what I'll do."

With that, he turned around, walked back to the beggar and asked, "Would you like these grapes?"

The beggar said without hesitation, "Yes."

The pastor said, "Here you are then," as he handed them over and continued on.

The thought went through his mind, "I wonder what that was all about." He concluded he didn't need to know. He had been prompted by the Holy Spirit to serve a fellow human being, and he had obeyed. That's all that mattered. That was enough for him. He was going where Jesus would go to do what Jesus would do.

That should be enough for us too. We should "hear" the Holy Spirit prompting us to love others and to do good deeds. In fact, we should be terrified if we do not. We should "do" what the Holy Spirit prompts us to do, even if it seems trivial or embarrassing. We just never know what God is doing. We don't have to. Our duty is simply to obey, not to explain.

Service should flow from hearts of gratitude that understand the grace of God in our lives, not as an expression of duty or as a means of bargaining to get something we want.

The Outworking of Faith

A relatively unknown Scandinavian bishop, Anders Nygren, once wrote a book titled *Agape und Eros*. In it he analyzed the biblical use of the two Greek words *agape* and *eros* to describe love.

Nygren discovered that *eros* love draws to itself egotistically, while *agape* love is outgoing and sacrificial. His book caught the attention of ethicists in the twentieth century, and it shifted the norm for ethics — what German theologian Helmut Thielicke called "the outworking of our Christian faith in the world" — from the *life* (or example) of Jesus to the *love* of Jesus.

To go where Jesus would go is to be guided by *agape* neighbor love. To do what Jesus would do is to be guided by *agape* neighbor love. It is *agape* love that will transform society.

Making *Agape* Choices

Standing out from all the other buildings in the middle of London today stands a soot-blackened church. Until the late 1960s all buildings in London looked the same, because all of London was heated by coal.

Since then, however, coal burning has been prohibited within a fifteen-mile radius of London. One by one the buildings have been cleaned, each owner responsible to clean their own building. Except this church. The declared mission of this church is to look after the poor on the streets. They believe that spending money to clean their church would detract from their mission. Consequently, it's unlikely the church will ever be cleaned.

Actually, this soot-covered church stands out as a powerful statement about the choices we make. There is certainly nothing more spiritual about the choice they've made. Another church can readily have a mission that calls for—even demands—a clean building. Yet it does reflect a keen awareness of the way in which they understand their calling to "go where Jesus would go to do what Jesus would do." Their choice reflects an intentionality about transforming "their" society with *agape* love.

The Object of Our Focus

It's said that motorcycle policemen are trained to avoid looking at the car they're pursuing when winding around a curve. If they do, they will be drawn toward the car on which they have focused and they will run off the road. Instead, they are trained to keep their eyes on the road immediately ahead.

We too are drawn toward that on which we focus. When we take our eyes off the narrow road of surrender, obedience, and service, we too run the risk of swerving off the road.

A lot of us are disappointed with the way our lives seem to be turning out. For some of us, we've forgotten why we're here, and that's why we are disappointed. We took our eyes off the road. We've run ourselves into a ditch.

Man Serving God

Ethicist James Gustafson once made the observation that the practice of the slogan "God serving man" was tearing society apart. We often live, he noted, as though the very reason for God's existence is to serve man—running errands for him. The end result is a pathetically low view of God. We must return to the practice of the maxim "man serving God." What would it look like for a man to go where Jesus would go and do what Jesus would do?

A survey of the New Testament Gospels will reveal that Jesus engaged in three primary activities:

◆ **He relieved human suffering.**

◆ **He taught people about the kingdom of God.**

◆ **He trained disciples to do what he did.**

Some "ministry" is organized. In every community and church, people who are committed to a ministry of good deeds have been mobilized and sent out to help homeless, poor, pregnant, uneducated, indigent, imprisoned, broken, disabled, diseased, unemployed, and hungry people.

You can easily take advantage of your connections to learn about these outreach opportunities. You can contribute money or labor. My wife, for example, tutors at a home for teenagers struggling to cope with life. You could serve on a board—most local ministries are in desperate need of individuals who are skilled leaders in organizational administration.

Most ministry, though, is like green grapes—it just happens. A small child in our community recently was reported missing. Over one hundred people turned out to "minister" to the family by searching for the child.

Most ministry is simply interacting with your "neighbors" along the path of life you travel. A man once asked Jesus, "And who is my neighbor?" Jesus responded by telling the parable of the Good Samaritan (see Luke 10:25−37). The essence of his teaching is this: Our neighbor is anyone whose need we see, whose need we are in a position to meet. If you have green grapes and feel motivated to give them away, just do it!

B. B. Warfield, a Princeton scholar and theologian, was one of the greatest minds of the twentieth century. He helped preserve conservative, orthodox faith against the attacks of liberalism in the church.

This brilliant man was loved and respected for his service to the church, but he "served" his wife in an even more profound way. On their honeymoon Warfield's wife had been struck by lightning. For the rest of his life he took care of her, carrying her daily up and down the stairs—serving her with love and compassion.

God invites us into a process of growing in relationship with him and with others. Interact with life right where you are, just as it occurs. Don't hold out to serve God until you finally get the life you wish you had.

What About Bob?

A man I know, a man named Bob, is a retired engineer who bounds around with endless energy.

"What time do you get up?" I asked him one day.

"I get up at 5:00 A.M. every day," he answered.

I was taken aback. "Why in the world do you get up at five o'clock? I thought all retired people got up at 7:30?" I responded.

He came back with this remarkable statement: "God has put this desire in my heart about things that need to be done." Bob has now challenged over two hundred men to meet in pairs once a week for prayer. He has started thirteen small-group Bible studies.

He has certainly made a sacrifice to serve. Yet, Bob would say that the reward has far exceeded the cost.

In New Testament times the Greek mind viewed service as *menial;* the Jewish mind viewed their service as somehow *meritorious;* but to the Christian mind service was to be, above all else, *sacrificial.*

Serving does cost us something. It is a sacrifice. It means to follow Jesus—to go where he would go to do what he would do. Jesus said, "Whoever serves me must follow me; and where I am, my servant also will be" (John 12:26).

Serving is also its own reward. It is the purest source of joy and honor imaginable. Jesus went on to express this stunning conclusion: "My Father will honor the one who serves me" (John 12:26).

Where Would Jesus Go?

One day our daughter sat next to a young man on an airplane. She struck up a conversation that eventually turned to the subject of homosexuality. At one point he admitted to her, "I'm very homophobic."

Our daughter, a deeply spiritual and thoughtful person, said "Really? Well, you know if Jesus were here, that's exactly the kind of people he'd be hanging out with."

The young man retorted, "That's not right! You don't know Jesus. He would never hang out with those kind of people."

She looked at him and laughed and said, "What Bible are you reading?"

In his life here on earth where did Jesus go? Except for the geography in which he operated, Jesus knew no other boundaries. His focus, however, was singular. He focused on spiritually and physically needy people.

Jesus hung out with three kinds of people:

◆ *Religious* people, like Nicodemus (see John 3)

◆ *Secular* people, like Zacchaeus (see Luke 19)

◆ *Broken* people, like Bartimaeus (see Mark 10)

Religious people, secular people, and broken people. Jesus went to rich and poor, weak and strong, religious and pagan. Jesus hung out with people who had prostituted their bodies as well as those who had prostituted their souls. Jesus hung out with anybody who wanted to talk about the kingdom. That's where he went when he lived here on earth so many years ago.

Where would Jesus go today? In the cathedrals of commerce where CEOs have become our high priests, there we would find Jesus. In the nursing homes where the elderly reside, so often lonely and forgotten, there we would find Jesus. Jesus would feel just as comfortable sleeping under an overpass as he would riding in a stretch limo.

We should be suspicious of our commitment to be followers of Jesus when we don't interact with a balance of religious, secular, and broken people who need a healing touch from Jesus—for body, mind, or soul.

In every place Jesus might visit today he would want to know, "Where is the sting of the lack of the gospel felt in this place? Where are the hurting people? Where are the people with AIDS? Where are the kids on drugs? Where are the businessmen about to fail? Where is the little teenage girl who has just had an abortion? Where can I find these people? Where are they, because I want to be where they are."

What would Jesus do when he got there? He would relieve their suffering. He would talk about the kingdom. He would tell his disciples to do what he was doing.

Do What You Can Do

Once I hired a new secretary who was experiencing a lot of turmoil in her private life. I knew that to be the case when I hired her.

One day as I was speaking to her about other matters I said, "Mary, I know something of how much pain you're going through in your life right now. I feel that God has called me to help you. [What I meant was I believed I had a call to 'serve' her, though I didn't use that word.]

"Let me tell you how I think God is calling me to help you. I think he is calling me to give you a place where you can work and have some dignity restored to your life." She had been through a divorce, and we all know how self-esteem typically gets trampled in a divorce. She needed some sense of dignity in her life. She needed to feel good about herself.

And then I said, "And what's more, Mary, I can give you a place where you can earn a fair wage" (because she's now the head of a household). That was something very tangible I could do for her.

"When we interact," I continued, "I'm not going to take an hour every day to ask you how it's going, how you're doing. I'm not going to do that. You're going to need to find that kind of support somewhere else, because if I did that, you wouldn't get the things done that pay the salary so you can have the dignity and the income, okay?"

The point of this small story is this: We do what we can do, right where we are, with the resources we've been given. And then we trust God's providence to do the rest. We are not the saviors of the whole world, but we are servants in the world God places before us. We do what we can do by going where Jesus would go to do what Jesus would do.

There's an old story that expresses the reality of God's call to join him in serving humanity, and it goes like this: A man was standing before God. The man's heart was breaking because of all the pain and suffering he saw in the world. And he cried out, "Dear God! I see all this pain and suffering. Why don't you send someone?" God answered, "I did. I sent you."

FOCUS QUESTIONS

1. When you look at your own life situation, do you see "God serving man" or "man serving God"? Explain your answer.

2. "A lot of us are disappointed with the way our lives seem to be turning out. For some of us, we've forgotten why we're here, and that's why we are disappointed." To what extent does this describe you and why?

3. "It is by taking the narrow road of giving that we end up on the broad road of receiving." Do you agree or not, and why? Have you been wondering, "What's the point?" If so, how could this vision of "service" help get you back on a right track?

4. This observation was made: *A servant is someone who goes where Jesus would go to do what Jesus would do.* Where would Jesus go? What would Jesus do? Where should you go, and what should you do?

5. Take a moment to jot down the names of a religious person, a secular person, and a broken person you know. What specifically can you do to serve them in the days ahead?

CHAPTER NINE

SOME HELIUM FOR
YOUR BALLOON

9

SOME HELIUM FOR YOUR BALLOON

Two things heal especially—a tear and a good laugh.

American evangelist Billy Sunday once said, "I pity anyone who can't laugh. There must be something wrong with their religion or with their lives." The famous Protestant reformer Martin Luther went even further: "If you're not allowed to laugh in heaven, I don't want to go there."

What is the problem humor solves? Simply put, humor is an antidote for stress and boredom, and a secret to long life. The youthfulness of my eighty-one-year-old accountability partner astounds his doctors. One day a doctor asked him, "Mr. Moar, how is it that a man your age can have so much fun?" Ken attributes his joy to a relationship with Jesus Christ and a good sense of humor.

Stress

Recently I was waiting in line at a specialty coffee store to purchase a muffin and cup of coffee. Each order was custom-made, which, of course, takes more time than prepackaged fare. For the entire five minutes I stood in line a man behind me was complaining. He said things like, "I can't believe how slow these people are. What's taking so long? Can't they speed things up?" and on and on. He was definitely wearing his underwear too tight.

We do seem to be in more of a hurry than ever before. Life feels more urgent, more threatening. We can spend too much time in emergency mode. The accumulated pressure takes its toll on body and soul.

Technically, for the last sixty years or so, the emergency response has been called the "fight-or-flight" syndrome. Here's what happens to your body in this mode:

When you perceive a danger your pituitary gland secretes a hormone called adrenocorticotropic which causes your adrenal gland to release other hormones. These adrenal hormones—adrenaline (epinephrine) and cortisol—immediately cause your pulse to quicken, your muscles to tense, and your blood pressure to increase. Your body is made ready to fight or flee.

During an emergency you need more blood in your large muscles, so your heart beats faster and your blood pressure increases abruptly. Also, blood is directed away from your stomach and skin. Your body releases more fat into the bloodstream because fat is an excellent quick source of energy. Your blood sugar concentration increases for the same reason. Your body secretes chemicals that make it easier for your blood to clot in case of an injury.

Your nervous system also is brought into action so that the pupils of your eyes dilate to permit better vision. Your facial muscles become tense, possibly to look more menacing. Perspiration increases to keep your body cool. Respiration accelerates to increase the oxygen available to your blood.

These changes prepare your body for emergencies, both real and imagined.[1]

1. David E. Larson, Editor-in-Chief, *Mayo Clinic Family Healthbook* (New York: Morrow, 1990), 400.

This amazing miracle of how the body responds to threats comes from God. But it is meant to serve as a defense mechanism, not as a way to live your life day in and day out.

Too much time in the foxhole creates accumulated stress. Stress will not only worsen but even produce symptoms when the demands on you outweigh your resources to cope with them.[2] Some suggest that the majority of doctor visits can be traced back to the effects of accumulated stress—perhaps as much as ninety percent according to some estimates.

Humor is one way to address the problem of stress. God gives us adrenaline to protect us from too much danger, and humor to protect us from too much adrenaline.

SECRET #9
HUMOR

Everyone enjoys a good laugh — or ought to.

Humor is the oil God squirts on our troubles to lubricate the friction. Humor is how God tickles a world that takes itself so seriously. The world boils and roils inside a pressure cooker; humor trips the release valve.

Like helium in balloons, humor lightens things up. Humor changes the physics of interpersonal gravity. Like a crash diet, humor quickly lightens up a moment that has become too heavy. It lets you slip a point in the side door. It lets you communicate serious points in a nonconfrontational way.

Humor can build a bridge, or tear down a wall. It can bring down the proud, or raise up the downtrodden. It's an escape route from awkward situations. It's a break in dark clouds that lets a beam of light shine down. It is a mirror that lets you see yourself as others do — and so to laugh a bit.

---

2. Larson, *Mayo Clinic Family Healthbook*, 400.

The late British writer and social critic Malcolm Muggeridge once said, "There is a close connection between clowns and mystics. . . . Laughter, indeed, is God's therapy; he planted the steeples and the gargoyles, gave us clowns as well as saints, in order that we might understand that at the heart of our mortal existence, there lies a mystery, at once unutterably beautiful and hilariously funny."[3]

The Walt Disney Company understands. It has a simple formula for successful movies: *Make them laugh and make them cry.*

What Humor Is

There are three kinds of people in the world—those who can count and those who can't. A lot of humor erupts out of the incongruent and unexpected.

Anyone who travels much in the Southeast region of the United States invariably ends up making plane connections through the Atlanta airport. Passing through Atlanta many times each year, I've settled into a routine. I'm used to taking the underground train and, almost before the doors fully open, hearing the "Darth Vader" voice announce, "Stop! Do not enter! The doors will not reopen!"

One day as I boarded the train, "Darth" made his announcement, and then he said something I had never heard before: "Caution, something is caught in the door! Please remove it immediately!"

In the middle of his sentence, the train lurched forward and left the station. A fellow traveler deadpanned, "Never mind. It doesn't make any difference, because we're leaving now anyway." It was an unexpected incident, and everyone on the train burst into laughter.

---

3. Cal and Rose Samra, *Holy Humor* (New York: Guideposts, 1996), xiv—xv.

The incongruent and unexpected can range from an all-out belly buster to the merely amusing. What is the most famous painting in the world? Why? Isn't it because of the amused smile on her face?

Humans have an almost infinite variety of ways of expressing humor. When we use *irony*, we essentially say one thing while meaning another—a deliberate contrast or incongruity between the stated and intended meaning. The man who coordinates the Bible study I teach in Orlando rarely remembers to bring his Bible. Over the years I've teased him often, mostly because it gets a laugh. One day he actually brought his Bible to a meeting, so I said, "Jim, I'm so proud of you for bringing your Bible today." Everyone knew that wasn't my true meaning, so they laughed.

Sometimes we use *sarcasm*, which is irony with a little more bite to it, often meant to cut or to wound. For example: "That's a great suit. Too bad they didn't have your size."

To express *wit* is to make a clever comment that shows a similarity between seemingly dissimilar things. One day I got a good laugh when I said, "My hairline's receding, but at least I don't have to worry about that cowlick anymore."

Satire exposes or pokes fun at human weaknesses. A man I work with came up with this bumper "snicker" idea:

Baptists: Smile, God loves you.

Presbyterians: Smile, God may love you.

Catholics: Smile, God loves you. Keep up the good work.

Done well, humor is a beautiful gift of God. What is the problem that humor solves? Holy humor is a taste of heaven that heals our present pain. Humor is *heavenly, holy,* and *healing.*

Humor Is Heavenly

Take a mental snapshot of how your insides feel when you laugh. That's a foretaste of the perpetual joy of heaven.

God is a funny God. The next time you go shopping at the mall glance around at the curious bodies people occupy and the funny ways they dress, then try to stifle a chuckle or see if you can keep that amused smile from spreading all across your face.

How can I make the claim that humor is grounded in God? According to the Bible, God creates times to laugh: "There is a time for everything, and a season for every activity under heaven . . . a time to weep and a time to laugh" (Ecclesiastes 3:1, 4).

In his own ministry Jesus made lavish use of humor to make a point and drive it home, particularly the technique called *hyperbole*, or extravagant exaggeration. He talked about moving mountains into the sea (Matthew 17:20) and camels going through the eyes of needles (Matthew 19:24). Today he might say, "It would be easier to get a refund from the Internal Revenue Service than for a rich man to enter the kingdom of heaven."

What will heaven be like? In its simplest, and perhaps its most profound, terms, heaven will be a place of perpetual joy. The Bible tells us that in heaven there will be no more mourning or crying (see Revelation 21:4).

Jesus came to give us "intermediate" joy on earth. God is not only our creator and redeemer, but he is our sustainer. Humor is one of the many means he uses to sustain us over the course of our lives here on earth. Humor, then, is a foretaste of heaven, an hors d'oeuvre, a snack to tide us over, an appetizer in anticipation of the main course.

Holy humor is a foretaste of heaven that heals our present pain. Humor, as we have seen, is heavenly; we'll now see that it is also holy.

Humor Is Holy

Because humor is from God it must be kept wholesome. The apostle Paul counsels, "Nor should there be obscenity, foolish talk or coarse joking, which are out of place, but rather thanksgiving" (Ephesians 5:4). Beyond that, the wise man Solomon offers this sage advice: "It is silly to be laughing all the time" (Ecclesiastes 2:2, NEW LIVING TRANSLATION).

Almost every beautiful gift from God can be distorted—gifts like sex, prosperity, power, and even humor. How can humor be denigrated? Humor that causes someone to blush in embarrassment, exploits someone's weakness in order to obtain a laugh, invokes profanity, uses vulgarity, or excludes someone from joining in the laughter can be considered inferior humor and in most cases inappropriate humor.

Here's a good rule of thumb: If someone can't be present during times of laughter or joking, that humor is not holy.

Holy humor is a foretaste of heaven that heals our present pain. Humor is not only heavenly and holy; it is also healing.

Humor Is Healing

Once I invited several leading black pastors to my office for lunch to explore the possibility of hosting a citywide men's event for our community.

For whatever reason, however, on the morning of the luncheon I spent time in prayer, and I found myself uttering these words: "Lord, I really have no agenda but you. Show me how I can serve these men."

At lunch these men deeply enjoyed each other's company, and the idea of a men's event never seemed appropriate to bring up. Instead, they expressed a desire to get to know their counterparts in the major white churches of our city. Those white pastors responded to the initial invitation to come together, and so we proceeded to meet again several times.

One day, after sharing funny war stories and hilarious bloopers, I asked them, "Where do you men want this gathering to go?" To a man they all said that what was taking place was exactly what they needed. It was a pressure valve. Nothing could help them more than to have a good laugh with their peers.

Consider these nuggets of wisdom from Scripture:

- ◆ A cheerful heart is good medicine, but a crushed spirit dries up the bones (Proverbs 17:22).

- ◆ A happy heart makes the face cheerful (Proverbs 15:13).

- ◆ The cheerful heart has a continual feast (Proverbs 15:15).

- ◆ A cheerful look brings joy to the heart (Proverbs 15:30).

The healing powers of laughter have been documented by Norman Cousins in *The Anatomy of an Illness*. The apostle Paul used humor to take the sting out of difficult situations. Once when he was facing opposition he released the pressure by saying, "As for those agitators, I wish they would go the whole way and emasculate themselves!" (Galatians 5:12).

On the occasion of turning ninety-five, Bob Hope shared the secret to his longevity. "Everyone tells you it's diet and exercise," he said. "But laughter is it. Laughter is therapy—an instant vacation."

Be Funny

It's doubtful that you can be happy without a healthy dose of humor. If you are not a particularly happy man, could humor help? Why not consider cultivating a more humorous disposition. Look for humor in the situations that ordinarily make you frustrated or angry.

If you are not a particularly funny person, make some funny friends, watch funny television shows, or rent funny movies. You can't change reality, but you can diffuse it.

Use humor as an expression of love. My wife often puts an unexpected note in an unexpected place. These notes make me smile and remind me of how great it is to be loved. One day I ran out of honey, so I added an item to the shopping list Patsy keeps in the kitchen: "Honey, honey." ☺ I don't know if she found any humor in it, but I sure did as I wrote it.

My publisher, Zondervan Publishing House, has a Humor Committee. At the beginning of one summer a few years ago the committee gave a goldfish to each department. The object was to foster a loving, caring environment and see how many goldfish would still be alive by the end of summer. Each department was asked to name its fish, and a prize was offered for coming up with the best story about their fish's life at Zondervan. The last department with a live fish would win the grand prize.

Within days goldfish began to disappear. The fishnappers sent ransom notes by e-mail. Some departments put their goldfish together so they wouldn't get lonely and die. Everyone had a super time and, through the use of humor, the world at Zondervan became a better place to work.

Let me conclude this chapter with this thought from one of the world's great philosophers, Yogi Berra. The former star catcher for the New York Yankees once said, "Always be sure to go to other people's funerals. Otherwise they won't go to yours."

Focus Questions

1. **What is the funniest thing that has happened to you recently?**

2. **What kind of humor do you enjoy the most? Why?**

3. **Humor is h_____ (Isaiah 61:3; 65:13–19). How does humor, like an hors d'oeuvre, give a foretaste of everlasting heavenly joy? How can you use humor to turn your thoughts toward heaven?**

4. **Humor is h_____ (Ephesians 5:4). Because humor is from God it must be kept wholesome. Like the beautiful gifts of prosperity and sex, the gift of humor can be distorted. How can humor be denigrated? Are**

there some changes you need to make in order to keep your humor holy?

5. Humor is h_____ (Proverbs 17:22). How has humor been "good medicine" for you and your family? Is there anything you can do to make it more so?

6. What is one practical step you can take to make humor a more common characteristic of your own happy life?

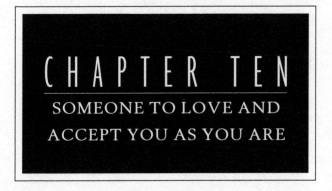

CHAPTER TEN

SOMEONE TO LOVE AND
ACCEPT YOU AS YOU ARE

SOMEONE TO LOVE AND
ACCEPT YOU AS YOU ARE

On a Sunday morning some time ago we celebrated communion in our home church and received the bread and juice a few rows behind an elderly couple. After the trays of bread had been passed, our pastor announced, "When the tray of grape juice comes to you, remove one of the small cups and pass on the tray."

As the tray approached the couple seated in front of us, the little old man removed a communion cup, drank from it, but placed the empty cup back into a slot in the tray. His wife whispered in his ear, undoubtedly something like: "You're not supposed to put the empty cup back in the tray."

Whatever she said, he obviously misunderstood her, because he promptly removed another cup, drank from it as well, and placed the second empty cup in the tray. His wife didn't say another word. She removed his two empty cups and a cup for herself, then passed the tray down the row. Her husband never did understand what happened.

As I watched this tender moment, I found myself fighting back tears because of the loving way this woman overlooked the weakness in her mate of "who-knows-how-many" years.

She loved him with the love of Jesus. I know in my heart that God was pleased with her at that moment. Isn't God good? And isn't it wonderful when we accept each other for what we are?

God loves that feeble old man. God loves him just the way he is. And isn't it wonderful that his wife is wise enough to love him that way too. I could not help but think to myself, *That's the way I want to love. That's the way I want to be loved.*

The Power of Love

In the movie *As Good As It Gets* actor Jack Nicholson portrays an abrasive author with Obsessive-Compulsive Disorder who won't take his pills. He doesn't want anyone except actress Helen Hunt, a divorced waitress struggling to make ends meet, to wait on him.

He falls in love with her and makes blundering attempts to win her affections in return. But he repeatedly alienates her with insensitive and often cruel remarks.

After engineering a road trip to help a mutual friend, they go on what could barely be called a dinner date. She finally begins to warm up to him, but she wonders out loud if he can muster a compliment.

He considers this thought for a moment, then tells her, "I started taking the pills."

She has no idea what he means. So to explain himself he says with great feeling, "You make me want to be a better man."

By God's grace, my greatest strength is that I'm married to someone who accepts and loves me just as I am. My express purpose in this chapter is to show you a foolproof formula to find that kind of love — the kind of love that will both anchor and liberate your heart.

Secret #10
Love

Though we create vast technologies that link together the whole world, though we discover miraculous cures for deadly plagues, though we erect tall buildings to celebrate the lofty heights of human achievement, inside the breast of every man is a little boy who from time to time becomes terrified by the uncertainties of what an unseen future holds, a little child who longs to curl up and be held close in the loving arms of someone who really cares.

At the end of the day, we are all weak people who need other weak people to love us, not so much for what we can become — for our potential — but because of who we are right now, and in spite of what we have done or have failed to do. If someone will love us like this, we will experience the joy of the Lord. We will find ourselves wanting to be "a better man." And if not, we are destined to spend our days longing for love. "It is not good for the man to be alone" (Genesis 2:18).

The Problem

Here is a truth that is beyond dispute: Men are either *fulfilled, frustrated,* or *failing* in love.

Recently I watched two young women in their early twenties waiting for a store to open. Their appearance was hard, not soft. They puffed on their cigarettes, and their body language communicated in a streetwise way that said, *You'd better not mess with me.* I remember feeling so sad, and thinking, *These girls have never known a father's unconditional love.*

That scene stands in sharp contrast to scenes from the life of a young man named Walt, a statewide high school track star. Walt's father, a highly successful attorney, made it his business to never miss a meet. Walt's dad always asked for his track schedule at the beginning of the school year so he could schedule the meets into his calendar. Walt never understood why having those dates so early was important until years later when he himself became a busy executive.

Because Walt was diligent in practice he developed powerful, well-conditioned legs. One day those muscular legs carried him to victory at a major state track meet. The crowd roared as he crossed the finish line. As he looked around he saw his dad making his way toward him. He so appreciated the way his father was always there for him—win or lose. His father's love seemed extra-special that day, especially as he watched his dad use his crutches to drag his polio-stricken legs across the field.

To be fulfilled in love is to experience what poet Robert Frost called "an irresistible desire to be irresistibly desired." If you are fulfilled in love, you have someone, somewhere, who makes you feel wanted. It will probably be your wife, if married. If not, it may be a friend, a child, or a parent. Or, if you have been truly blessed, you will be loved by more than one person.

Many men, though, are frustrated in love.

Take Dennis, for example. Dennis and his wife both work. Dennis goes out of his way to share household chores. She goes out of her way to spend time with him.

However, she doesn't offer Dennis much help with simple errands like picking up his shirts from the laundry, which makes him get cranky. Conversely, he seems too tired most days to spend quiet times together with her, which makes her feel "unconnected."

Author Gary Chapman helps us understand a little better the dynamics at work in our relationships, pointing us to the remarkable insight that husbands and wives tend to love each other the way *they* want to be loved, but not necessarily the way their *mates* want to be loved.

The problem Dennis faces is that he is loving his wife the way he wants to be loved, but not the way she wants to be loved. Because he would feel more loved if she were more of a "helper," he assumes she will feel more loved if he is more of a "helper" to her. This assumption leads to frustration. She would actually feel more loved if he would spend more time with her in meaningful conversation.

The problem Dennis's wife faces is that she is loving Dennis the way she wants to be loved, but not the way to which he best responds. Because she would feel more loved if he would spend time with her, she assumes he will feel more loved if she spends time with him. This assumption leads to frustration. Dennis would actually feel more loved if she would offer more help with errands and chores.

While some men are *fulfilled* and others are *frustrated,* many more are actually *failing* in love. Recently one of my coworkers received a phone call from his neighbor. The night before the neighbor had lost his temper, yanked the phones out of the wall in his home, then left. Terrified, his wife had called the police. He called my friend the next morning because he wanted someone to accompany him to the police station where he would turn himself in.

Most men have enough unresolved anger that stories like this frighten us a bit. We realize that if not for God's grace at work to restrain us, we could all too easily lose control ourselves. In fact, some of us have.

Whether you are fulfilled, frustrated, or failing in love, love is the glue that will hold our lives together and the oil that will keep us from rubbing each other the wrong way. Let's look now at the secret of how we can be genuinely happy in love.

The Riddle of Love

Here is the riddle of love: *Someone will love you as you are when you love them as they are because Christ loves you as you are.* This riddle has three parts; the first, the fundamental, part is the last clause of the riddle.

CHRIST LOVES YOU AS YOU ARE.

Someone has already loved you as you are. The starting point for any meaningful discussion about love is Jesus Christ.

My calling, received in 1987, is "to take God's message of love to a broken generation." For the first nine years of this calling I studied contemporary culture and grew to understand something of how and why we live in a broken generation. Yet "God's message of love" remained an elusive mystery to me. All those years I pleaded and prayed for God to show me the message of his love.

One day, unexpectedly, as I was reading 1 John 4:9–10 the scales fell from my eyes. The thought sprang into my mind: *Jesus Christ is God's message of love.* "That's it!" I exclaimed. "It's just that simple!"

Indeed, Jesus Christ is God's message of love to us who live in a broken generation. Listen to how the Bible puts it: "This is how God showed his love among us: He sent his one and only Son into the world that we might live through him. This is love: not that we loved God, but that he loved us and sent his Son as an atoning sacrifice for our sins" (1 John 4:9–10).

The love of Christ is *agape* love. It is compassionate, sacrificial, gracious, and unconditional.

The compassionate love of Jesus Christ engages your hurts. When Jesus went off to be alone and pray (see Luke 5:16), he didn't say to those who came to him seeking help, "I can't believe you're interrupting my quiet time! Now go on, get out of here." The love of Jesus isn't irritated with you. His love is not judgmental. His love is characterized by compassion.

The *sacrificial* love of Jesus Christ gives up something for you. In baseball a "sacrifice" results when the batter hits a ball, expecting to be called out, but advancing a runner to the next base. That's the kind of love Jesus offers us. He voluntarily gave up what was rightfully his, "making himself nothing" as the apostle Paul writes in Philippians 2:7, so we could advance to Home Plate. His love is characterized by sacrifice. He gave up his life for us.

The *gracious* love of Jesus Christ cancels what we do deserve and gives us what we don't deserve. What does he cancel that we do deserve? By his mercy he cancels the punishment we deserve. What does he give us that we don't deserve? By his grace he forgives our sin and gives us the gift of eternal life. The Bible puts it this way: "When you were dead in your sins and in the uncircumcision of your sinful nature, God made you alive with Christ. He forgave us all our sins" (Colossians 2:13). His love is wonderfully gracious.

The *unconditional* love of Jesus Christ accepts us even as "continual" sinners, as long as we admit it: "If we claim we have not sinned, we make him out to be a liar and his word has no place in our lives" (1 John 1:10).

In sports you have to be good enough in your athletic skill to make the team. In business you have to perform according to agreed-on standards in order to keep your job. In society you have to be a winner in order to merit recognition. In Jesus Christ, you do not have to be good enough, you do not have to perform, you do not have to be a winner. Ironically, to be in Christ means exactly the opposite—it is to admit that you are not good enough, that you cannot perform, that because of sin's grip on your life you are a loser—and to admit, for that very reason, that you need a Savior, a Savior whose unconditional love transforms your life.

I believe this is what God wants to say to men today about love: *The pressure is off. This is not an athletic performance. You do not have to be good enough for me to love you. Nothing you can do will make me love you less. In fact, nothing you can do will make me love you* more. *I love you just as you are, for what you are, with all your faults and frailties.*

Even if no one else steps forward to love you, Jesus loves and accepts you as you are. That's the first and fundamental part of the riddle.

LOVE OTHERS AS THEY ARE

Second, you love others as they are.

Love is the most powerful force in the world. Consider this beautiful story of what can happen when we love others as Christ loves us. A Wycliffe Bible translator, Doug Meland, and his wife moved among the Fulnio Indians in Brazil. They called him simply "the white man." Yet, this was a term of derision because white men had plundered their lands and burned their homes.

As time passed the Melands learned the language and offered medical help to the Fulnio Indians. Eventually the people began to call him "the respectable white man."

In the same way that American General Norman Schwarzkopf received greater acceptance by the Saudis during the Gulf War when he dressed in Arab robes, the Melands found greater acceptance among the Fulnios when they started adopting Fulnio customs. In time the Fulnios began to call him "the white Indian."

Then one day Doug Meland stooped to wash the dirty, blood caked foot of an injured Fulnio Indian boy. A shocked bystander said to another, "Whoever heard of a white man washing an Indian's foot before? Surely this man is from God!"

From that day forward, whenever Doug Meland would enter the home of a Fulnio Indian, they would announce, "Here comes the man God sent."

Because Jesus loves you as you are, you are "commanded" to love others as they are. Take some time to let these Bible verses sink deep into your thinking:

Dear friends, since God so loved us, we also ought to love one another.

I JOHN 4:11

A new command I give you: Love one another. As I have loved you, so you must love one another.

JOHN 13:34

My command is this: Love each other as I have loved you. Greater love has no one than this, that he lay down his life for his friends.

JOHN 15:12–13

Loving Your Wife

If your wife is not as lovable as she once was, guess whose fault that is? A woman is a fragile flower, a special creature of God, made to become a partner with a man who will honor and respect and love her. That's certainly how every marriage starts out. Nobody marries someone they don't like! So what are some of the challenges that come along the way?

In Genesis 3:16 we find the key to marital struggles. As a consequence of mankind's fall, God said to women, "Your *desire* will be for your husband, and he will rule over you" (italics added). This word "desire" literally means "a desire bordering on disease." In other words, because of the Fall a woman's desire for her husband is subject to corruption. For example, she may become overly possessive of him. Or he may manipulate her.

If you're married, the woman your wife has become is, by degrees, the woman you made her to be. Sociologists suggest that there is much truth in the looking-glass theory, which says, quite simply, that we tend to become what the most important person in our lives thinks we are.

Because Jesus loves you as you are, you must love others as they are. That's the second part of the riddle. And it leaves us ready to ask, "What's the third part?"

SOMEONE TO LOVE YOU AS YOU ARE

Third, someone will love you as you are.

It proved to be a most interesting discovery. In doing some research in preparation for writing this chapter I was amazed to find not one single instance in the Bible where it is suggested that we seek the love of others. Not even once! Now I ask you, have you ever seen this verse?

You must find someone to love you (Neurotica 7:11).

The Bible never tells us that it's our responsibility to scour the earth for someone who will love and accept us as we are. Rather, the Bible shows us how to become the kind of person who will, as a by-product of being a loving person who is loved by Jesus, draw others to us.

That's the secret to the riddle of love. Someone will love you as you are when you love them as they are because Christ loves you as you are.

Are you fulfilled in love? If so, congratulations! By degrees, you have been able to love sacrificially, focusing more on giving than on getting. You have been able to love unconditionally—accepting your wife, if married, as she is. You have given her large doses of "emotional" love—first understanding how she wants to be loved, and then doing so. You have been able to communicate—helping her understand how you want to be loved, and offering positive feedback on a consistent basis.

Are you frustrated or failing in love? Could it be that you don't love your wife the way you thought you did, or, if you are not married, that you don't have someone to whom you have given yourself? As a result, here's what could happen to you unless you begin investing in love: You're going to be focused on your needs, not hers. You're going to make selfish choices. You're going to go cold in your marriage, your work, your relationship with God. You're not going to be happy. You will want a "do over."

But here's the deeper problem. You will think a "do over" means a different chance in a different game. The truth is this: In God's economy, a "do over" means a second chance *in the same game*. The task before us is to love our wives in such a way that they are released to love us in return.

What If You're Not Loved

The story of Chad is heartbreaking and sad. Some time ago, Chad's wife asked for a divorce. He moved into an apartment; she stayed in the house with their five children. Two months later she called him, "If you will take the kids, I'll move into the apartment and you can move back into the house." That was four years ago, and she has shown no interest in Chad or the children since.

Some men reading this book have tried everything. They simply, like Chad, do not have a spouse or any other person right now who loves them as they are.

If you are lonely, by all means keep calling out to the God of love for a companion who will love and accept you as you are. In the meantime, accept this truth: A gracious Lord wants to immerse you in his love:

> *For I am convinced that neither death nor life, neither angels nor demons, neither the present nor the future, nor any powers, neither height nor depth, nor anything else in all creation, will be able to separate us from the love of God that is in Christ Jesus our Lord.*
>
> ROMANS 8:38–39

> *And I pray that you, being rooted and established in love, may have power, together with all the saints, to grasp how wide and long*

*and high and deep is the love of Christ, and to know this love that sur-
passes knowledge—that you may be filled to the measure of all the
fullness of God.*

EPHESIANS 3:17–19

Do Something Radical

With Jesus love is *radical* in the best sense of the word. In one passage alone he gives us seven radical things to do: love enemies, do good to those who hate us, bless those who curse us, pray for those who mistreat us, don't retaliate, give freely, and treat others the way we want to be treated (see Matthew 6:27–31).

If you want love, give love. Do something radical. Love the way Jesus loves.

I have a friend, Hunter, who has not spoken to his mother for over a year. A negative woman by disposition, she finally crossed the line and made some horrible remarks about Hunter's son, who had died of AIDS—and then proceeded to rip his wife pretty good too.

For over a year Hunter has been torn up inside. For all of her faults, she is still his mother. Yet he has felt deeply hurt and more bitter by the day. The emotional trauma was eating him alive.

One day in desperation he asked what he could do. I remarked, "Hunter, you can't change your mother. If that's your goal you will only become more and more upset. Furthermore, your mother's not getting any younger, and you probably need to chalk up some of her behavior to her age.

"There are two things you may want to seriously consider doing. First, make sure you and your wife are together on this. When a man marries, he 'leaves' his mother and father and 'cleaves' to his wife. Your first priority is your wife.

"Second, talk this over with your wife and see if you can find it in your hearts to forgive your mother and then make a decision to love and accept her just as she is, not as you'd like her to be. This may do nothing to change your relationship with her, or it may do everything. But even if it does nothing, you and your wife will feel a weight off your shoulders—a release. You will be liberated by Christ from the bondage you feel."

A week later Hunter called to say that a phone call he had made to his mother had gone poorly. However, before making the call he and his wife had prayed together and had decided to forgive his mother and accept her as she is. "Honestly," he said in a voice thick with emotion, "even though the relationship is still not right, Jesus *has* set us free."

FOCUS QUESTIONS

1. Do you have someone who loves and accepts you as you are? If so, to what do you attribute that? If not, what could be some of the reasons?

2. Are you *fulfilled, frustrated,* or *failing* in love? Why?

3. Do you love others the way they want to be loved, or do you still love others the way you wish they would love you?

4. Here is the riddle of love: *Someone will love you as you are when you love them as they are because Christ loves you as you are.* Which part of this statement have you been most successful in applying, and how so? Which part do you need to work on? What is something specific you can do today in that area?

5. Describe the love that Christ has for you. Describe the love that Christ commands you to have for others.

6. "If you're married, the woman your wife has become is, by degrees, the woman you made her to be." Do you agree with this statement? Why or why not? Can you think of something you want to do differently as a result of coming to see the truth of this claim?

7. Where is the following verse found in the Bible: "You must find someone to love you"? What are the implications for you personally of the point made in this chapter about this statement?

-Afterword-

Remember the description of the Honey Bell orange mentioned in the Introduction? I mentioned the Honey Bell orange because while writing these pages I found myself tasting the excellencies of Christ in a way that would make it difficult for me to ever again be satisfied with any ordinary happiness. I hope that by reading these pages you now feel the same.

We each need a book like this from time to time. Every day we get bombarded with messages about how to be happy. Sadly, these ideas rarely work out.

We can, however, find unimaginable happiness in unexpected places. Authentic, biblical Christianity ironically promises happiness as a reward for surrender and sacrifice. The happy Christian life is, in fact, counterintuitive. We saw this in the master secret:

> THE CHRISTIAN LIFE IS A BROAD ROAD OF HAPPINESS, JOY, PEACE, BLESSING, SUCCESS, SIGNIFICANCE, AND CONTENTMENT, WHICH IS IRONICALLY GAINED BY CHOOSING THE NARROW ROAD OF SURRENDER, OBEDIENCE, SELF-DENIAL, SELF-SACRIFICE, TRUTH, WORSHIP, AND SERVICE.

As we come to the end of our time together let me suggest two final ideas. First, it may be helpful to actually memorize the master secret. I have done so, and I find myself constantly referring to it as a focusing idea. It has been especially helpful when I'm making tough choices.

Second, listed below are summaries of the ten secrets we've covered. Why not take a moment right now and decide what changes, if any, you would like to make in each of those areas? I'm leaving a little room after each secret if you would like to jot down something.

◆ *Lordship* — Jesus Christ is the Lord of all men at all times in all places, whether they acknowledge it or not. We belong to Jesus. He is our "owner." He is our "benefactor." This is an idea that may take ten or twenty years to sink in.

◆ *Balance* — We can find what we're looking for by striking a right balance between the four universal purposes God has for all men: The Great Commandment, the New Commandment, the Cultural Mandate, and the Great Commission. It is the secret to leading a happy, busy, and balanced life.

◆ *Vocation* — A man who is unhappy in his work will find it difficult to be happy anywhere. For that reason, you should search for that occupation which, once discovered, you could be happy doing nothing else. At the same time, each of us must also remember that no amount of success at work can adequately compensate for failure at home.

◆ *Suffering* — Your sufferings are not merely setbacks. They are also springboards to the crucial task of knowing God well enough that you can trust him.

◆ *Discipleship* — Most of us have said, "I knew about God, but I didn't know God." Perhaps a greater problem today is that men do know God, but they don't know about him. To know God is to be a Christian. To know about God, however, is what it means to become a disciple.

◆ *Stewardship* — Stewardship is a total way of looking at life, which understands that everything comes from God, belongs to God, and is to be used for the glory of God. A steward will come to believe that God has a "plan" for his life — that God has ordained all his days before one of them came to pass, that God determines his times and even the exact places where he lives (see Psalm 139:16, Acts 17:26).

◆ *Witnessing* — The single most important need people have is to know Jesus Christ as their Savior and Lord. At the same time, few things in life are more nerve-racking than sharing our faith in Jesus Christ. Ironically, many men are dying to know what we are dying not to tell them. A true believer, however, will overcome these fears and feel a sense of urgency and responsibility to help men find faith. The happiest men in the world are witnessing Christians.

◆ **Service** — A servant is someone who goes where Jesus would go to do what Jesus would do. Where would Jesus go? What would Jesus do? Unless and until we serve him as an expression of gratitude our lives will have no enduring meaning. We will not be happy.

_____

_____

◆ **Humor** — Humor is how God tickles a world that takes itself so seriously. The world boils and roils inside a pressure cooker; humor trips the release valve. Humor can build a bridge, or tear down a wall. It is a mirror that lets you see yourself as others do — and so to laugh a bit.

_____

_____

◆ **Love** — At the end of the day, we are all weak people who need other weak people to love us, not so much for what we can become — for our potential — but because of who we are right now, and in spite of what we have done or failed to do. If someone will love us like this, we will experience the joy of the Lord.

_____

_____

You may have been surprised to learn that many of these secrets run against the grain of what you've heard "on the street" about life with God. That's because a lot of people are "tapping" in the wrong places. Knowing where to tap is the hard part—that's why it was worth $999 to the factory foreman in the end. In this book I have attempted to show you "where to tap" in order to find a deep, satisfying happiness. Now, let's go tapping.

-Patrick Morley-

Since the late 1980s, Patrick Morley has been one of America's most-respected authorities on the unique challenges and opportunities that men face. After spending the first part of his career in the highly competitive world of commercial real estate, Patrick has been used throughout the world to help men think more deeply about their lives.

In 1973 Patrick founded Morley Properties, which for several years was hailed as one of Florida's one hundred largest privately held companies. During this time he was the president or managing partner of fifty-nine companies and partnerships. In 1989 he wrote *The Man in the Mirror,* a landmark book that burst forth from his own search for meaning, purpose, and a deeper relationship with God. This best-selling book captured the imaginations of hundreds of thousands of men worldwide. As a result, in 1991, Patrick Morley sold his business and founded Man in the Mirror, a ministry to men. Through his speaking and writing, he has become a tireless advocate for men, encouraging and inspiring them to change their lives in Christ. He has now written eight books.

"Our ministry exists," says Patrick Morley, "in answer to the prayers of all those wives, mothers, and grandmothers who have for decades been praying for the men in their lives."

Man in the Mirror's faculty members conduct church-sponsored men's events nationwide. Patrick's dream is to network with other ministries and churches of all denominations to reach every man in America with a credible offer of salvation and the resources to grow in Christ.

Patrick Morley graduated with honors from the University of Central Florida, which selected him to receive its Distinguished Alumnus Award in 1984. He has completed studies at the Harvard Business School and Reformed Theological Seminary. Every Friday morning Patrick teaches a Bible study to 150 businessmen in Orlando, Florida, where he lives with his wife, Patsy, and his dog, Katie. Patrick and Patsy have two grown children.

Patrick's website can be found at: *www.maninthemirror.com*

-Acknowledgments-

A manuscript like this could never be the work of one author. Rather, these lessons are of a type that are gleaned by thousands of touches—large and small—of wise and godly people from the present, near past, and history.

Solomon wrote, "What has been will be again, what has been done will be done again; there is nothing new under the sun" (Ecclesiastes 1:9). That is certainly the case for this effort. For these reasons I would like to acknowledge a few of my debts.

From history: C. S. Lewis once said, somewhere, that for every new book you read you should also read an old book. This I have tried to do, though with limited success. However, I have been stimulated by ideas men and women have wrestled with for several millennia. I have tapped into that centuries-long conversation, and so would like to honor the great Christian thinkers and writers of history from whom I have learned so much, but realize that I could never specifically quote and honor appropriately. Thomas à Kempis, Augustine, Martin Luther, John Calvin, Brother Lawrence, Andrew Murray, Søren Kierkegaard, Dietrich Bonhoeffer, Oswald Chambers, C. S. Lewis, Francis Schaeffer, and the biblical writers come to mind.

From the near past: I would thank these men for their intentional and unintentional lessons: my father Bob Morley, my father-in-law Ed Cole, Hugh Lake, H. O. Giles, Dr. Gary Sowers, Jim Gillean, John Christiansen, Tom Skinner, Chuck Green, R. C. Sproul, and Bill Bright.

From the present: I am grateful for the lessons, encouragement, and support I continue to reap from my wife Patsy, daughter Jen, and son John. Also, the staff at Man in the Mirror, our board of directors, our faculty, the leaders at TGIF Men's Bible Study, my brothers in the National Coalition of Men's Ministries, Chuck Mitchell, and the pastors of my home church.

I would like to offer special appreciation to the team of professionals who brought this book from concept to final form: Robert Wolgemuth, Scott Bolinder, John Sloan, Dirk Buursma, John Topliff, Emily Klotz, Greg Stielstra, Robin Welsh, and a hundred others I have only heard about.